QUICK QUIPS
&
LONGER JOKES

A RACONTEUR'S DIRECTORY

Kevin Goldstein-Jackson

RIGHT WAY

Typeset in 11 pt Times by Letterpart Ltd. Reigate, Surrey.
Printed and bound in Great Britain by Cox & Wyman Ltd., Reading, Berkshire.

The *Right Way* series is published by Elliot Right Way Books, Brighton Road, Lower Kingswood, Tadworth, Surrey, KT20 6TD, U.K. For information about our company and the other books we publish, visit our web site at:
www.right-way.co.uk

CONTENTS

DEDICATION

This book is dedicated to my wife, Mei Leng, without whom I would not be married. Her assistance with *Quick Quips* has been considerable.

Quick Quips And Longer Jokes is also dedicated to all my friends, colleagues and acquaintances around the world who kindly made suggestions for it; and to Adam Young and my two daughters, Sing Yu and Kimberley, who vetted all the jokes for inclusion. My daughters have promised not to sue for mental cruelty. Sing Yu's assistance in sorting the jokes into categories was of great help.

This book is also dedicated, with much appreciation and thanks, to all the people who bought various editions of my other joke books in UK, US, Indian, Estonian, Japanese and other versions and thus created the demand for *Quick Quips And Longer Jokes*.

INTRODUCTION

Quick Quips And Longer Jokes has been designed not only to provide a humorous read, but also to be of use on a variety of occasions – whether they be business functions, drunken parties or those occasions when a quick quip or longer joke can act as a means of enlivening a speech or easing tension in a difficult situation or even 'putting someone in their place'.

All of the jokes have been written so that they can, if required, be spoken aloud without (unless you wish) having to change a word.

I have been writing, collecting and telling jokes since I was a small boy. At school I looked rather like a short, anorexic version of Harry Potter. This drew me to the attention of bullies. In such situations, a sense of humour can be useful in three different ways.

1. Telling good jokes is rather like having magical powers. Bullies can be disarmed, as those with a sense of humour will 'borrow' jokes to tell their friends and so are less likely to want to harm the source of the joke material.

2. Bullies tend to pick on people who show signs of fear. Having a sense of humour and looking at the funny side of difficult situations can help the fear to go away.

3. Despite the old saying: 'Sticks and stones may break my bones, but words can never harm me' – I have found that being able to make a 'put down' remark or other joke at a bully's expense will often make him/her avoid further confrontation. People generally do not like being laughed *at* – they may well remember a particularly cruel joke for far longer than a feeble punch or kick.

Humour can be helpful in all sorts of situations – from telling jokes to gain popularity, to using humour to make a difficult situation bearable.

For example, studies have shown that people with a sense of humour, who are ill, often have a better rate of recovery than people who are morose, brood on their illness and generally become depressed and give up hope.

In times of war, being able to make fun of the 'enemy' reduces their perceived power. The enemy no longer appear invincible if they can appear as a joke.

The jokes in this book cover a wide variety of topics. They have been listed alphabetically under various subject headings – but sometimes it has been almost impossible to decide under which of several equally appropriate main headings a joke should appear. To assist in the finding of a suitable joke, there is also a *Joke Directory* that begins on page 10.

Even more topics can be covered by making small changes to a joke. For example, some jokes relating to a particular profession could also apply to another occupation.

I do not claim to have been the originator of every joke in this book. Some of them have been told to me by friends, relatives and people I met during my travels and they, in turn, may well have been e-mailed or told the jokes by someone else.

A number of the jokes can be made 'up-to-the-minute' to take account of today's events and personalities simply by changing the 'he' or 'she' or name in the joke to that of a real person currently in the news. Or you could mention a current news event and use it as a lead in to a particular joke that has some relevance to the news.

Take care in your choice of jokes. If you are asked to speak in public, ask about the type of person who will be in the audience. Will they be offended by certain types of joke?

For example, while one audience may be offended by 'naughty' jokes – and even by the use of the word 'shit' (vital to the punchline of at least one joke) – others may well love such humour.

It is no longer safe to assume that elderly folk dislike 'rude' jokes. Indeed the joke in this book about birds and a

Scotsman's kilt was told to me by an 81-year-old woman.

However, while some jokes in this book are blue, none of them contain really strong four-letter swear words. This is because it is often easier for a speaker (if he/she wishes) to *add* such words to a joke than it is to remember to take such words *out*.

Although the first part of the title of this book is *Quick Quips*, a number of the jokes are much longer. Such jokes could be useful if you are called upon at a party to perform a 'party piece' and you have no desire to sing or perform in some other way.

If you want to amuse young children, then the section *Questions For Kids* might be useful at a kids' party. A small prize could even be given to the first person who can shout out the answer to one (or more) of the questions.

If you are speaking at an event that might be reported by the press, then be especially careful. Beware of what Prince Philip, Duke of Edinburgh, called 'dentopedalogy'. He defined this as 'the science of opening your mouth and putting your foot in it' and added that he had 'been practising it for years'.

Try not to make jokes that are likely to create such an adverse reaction that some members of the audience complain to the press. Also, do *not* use jokes to disparage your own firm's products since your comments could attract newspaper headlines and your firm's sales could fall. Instead, you could consider using such jokes to run down your competitors.

Many people are nervous about speaking in public. For years, the advice to such people was: 'You'll feel more at ease if you imagine the audience are all naked' – presumably because a clothed speaker would feel less nervous and embarrassed than a 'nude' audience.

I know a man with a vivid imagination who followed such advice. He looked out at the audience and imagined them all naked. His imagination was so intense that seeing attractive people in the audience looking at him provoked a visible bodily reaction.

Fortunately, he was standing behind a large lectern at the time – but his speech turned into a lengthy ramble while he waited for his imagination to subside sufficiently to be able to walk off the stage.

I believe it is much better to imagine the audience are all sitting on toilets. Or to remember that many well-known, highly paid professional performers still get nervous before (and sometimes during) their public speech.

If you stumble in your speech, simply say something like: 'I knew I shouldn't have borrowed my wife's teeth.' Or say: 'Well, I *am* only a substitute for . . .' and mention the name of a famous person who is known for his dull comments or who has recently embarrassed him/herself in public. The audience should then warm to you.

But the best way to make sure a speech will be well received is to test it on someone first. Try it out on someone who will give you an honest opinion – and then make any necessary changes. Or you could record your speech rehearsal and then play it back. Are you bored by it? Does it go on for too long?

A friend of mine once went into a bar and heard a man shout 'Fifty-eight' and everyone fell about laughing.

Then a woman shouted. 'Eight hundred and thirty-six' and people laughed loudly.

My friend asked a barman why people were laughing at numbers. He replied that at the start of the evening he had shouted out the title of one of my joke books in which each joke is individually numbered.

Everyone in the bar had read the book so many times they knew all the jokes – so all they had to do was shout out the numbers and they would all recall the joke.

My friend decided to join in and shouted out: 'One hundred and sixty-seven.' There was a modest titter. He tried again. 'Three hundred and fifty.' There was silence.

'Why such a poor reaction?' asked my friend. 'The numbers came from the same book.'

'Simple!' said the barman, 'It's the way you said them . . .'

When making a speech – or just telling jokes – it is best to try to vary the tone of your voice and pause from time to time. Where appropriate, use facial expressions (raised eyebrows, etc) and hand gestures.

Happy joking!

KG-J

DIRECTORY

This directory is intended for people wanting to find a joke on a particular subject for a speech or some other occasion. In the directory, the numbers shown are the *joke numbers*, not page numbers.

Please do not limit your search just to one particular heading. For example, if you are searching for material for a speech to make at a wedding, then many categories as well as the 'wedding', 'bridegroom', 'dating', 'marriage', 'sex', 'boyfriends', 'girlfriends', 'husbands' and 'wives' categories may also include suitable jokes. The same applies to speeches at business lunches – it is best to browse a wide selection of categories. In addition, some jokes can be *made* suitable for your occasion simply by changing the sex or profession/occupation category of the person described in the joke.

A

ACCIDENTS

1. The driver of a lorry loaded with the latest edition of a thesaurus swerved to avoid a cat and crashed into a tree. The driver was reported as being stunned, shocked, jolted, taken aback by the unexpected, unanticipated, unpredicted, unforeseeable, unannounced, unheralded event, misfortune, bad luck accident.

✿

2. Unfortunately, he lost his left arm, left ear and left leg in an industrial accident. He's all right now.

✿

3. Trevor was driving along a country lane when he suddenly swerved to avoid a stray dog. Hurtling out of control, the car fell into a ditch, rolled on to its side and trapped Trevor behind his wheel.

Two cyclists, twins Simon and Duncan Ball, witnessed the accident and went to see if they could assist Trevor. Unable to open the car door, one of the twins said they could try and break the car windscreen and pull Trevor out of the car. Trevor was concerned he might get badly cut by the broken glass and suggested the twins should go to nearby farms and ask a farmer to use a tractor to pull the car out of the ditch. Simon and Duncan Ball then raced off to neighbouring farms.

Thus it was a farmer who eventually freed Trevor from the car – which was probably better than being pulled out by the Balls.

✿

ACCOUNTANTS

4. The young accountant was called into the office of the senior partner of the firm. 'Sit down,' said the senior partner. 'I have been examining your record since you joined the firm eighteen months ago. During that time there have been queries regarding the accuracy of your auditing work and suspicions that you have accepted bribes in order to overlook certain matters. You have also been accused of sleeping with a number of married female executives working for the firms which you have audited. Your expenses claims are unusually large and on close examination you appear to have claimed for the cost of hookers for senior male executives of some of the firms which we audit. Your conduct is morally appalling.'

'Oh,' said the rather stunned young accountant.

'But,' continued the senior partner, 'you have achieved the largest increase in fees to our firm of any of our members. I shall therefore suggest to the board that you receive a significant bonus and promotion.'

✿

5. His business is so crooked his accountants and auditors specialise in accounts deceivable.

✿

6. The very busty accountant's assistant can't add. But she can certainly distract.

✿

7. He's such a good accountant he has a tax loophole named after him.

✿

8. What do accountants suffer from that other people do not? Depreciation.

✿

9. The trouble with the auditing profession is that 95 per cent of its members give the others a bad name.

✿

ACTORS AND ACTRESSES
10. He's such a wooden actor that when he cries, the tears are sap.

✿

11. The young actor was very excited and phoned his father. 'Dad, I've just been given a contract for a new film. I play the part of a senior civil servant.'

'Oh!' replied the father. 'Aren't you disappointed you're not going to play someone intelligent?'

❂

12. The aspiring young British actress went to Hollywood to further her career and made love under the stars.

❂

13. The famous actor was staying at an expensive hotel in London. Some of his fans had waited outside the hotel for hours in the hope of catching a glimpse of the man they adored.

Suddenly, accompanied by several bodyguards, he appeared in the foyer. The fans rushed towards him, but the security guards pushed them aside and escorted the actor to a limousine which rapidly drove him away.

Many of the fans were disappointed and went home. But several stayed in the hope of seeing him again – and possibly getting an opportunity to tell him how much they admired him.

Five hours later the actor returned. The fans walked rapidly towards him, some holding out their autograph books. The actor looked at them as he walked into the hotel and he sneered: 'What, *still* here? What kind of *creeps* are you? I haven't got time to waste on morons!'

This so annoyed one teenage fan that she punched him. Thus it really became the day when the fan hit the shit.

❂

14. The actress had just moved into the area and was registering her children with the local doctor. 'I've got five children – all boys,' she told the doctor's receptionist.

'First name?' asked the receptionist.

'They're all called George,' replied the woman.

The receptionist was surprised. 'Each of them has the first name George?' she asked.

'Yes,' replied the actress.

'But what happens when you call out "George" – how do they know which one you want?'

'That's easy. I've been married five times and they've each got a different surname so I use that.'

❀

ADAM AND EVE

15. Eve was in the Garden of Eden and thanked God for creating all the animals. However, she saw that the animals were having fun and enjoying sex, so she asked God if she could have similar companionship, too.

'OK,' said God. 'But if I create a male companion for you – let us call him Adam – you have to promise me that you won't tell him I created you first.'

❀

16. The reason that God created Man before he created Woman is because He wanted a rough draft before He made perfection.

❀

17. Adam in the Garden of Eden was getting rather bored talking to the plants and animals. 'Couldn't I have another human to talk to?' he asked God.

'Well,' said God, 'I could create a woman.'

'What's that?' asked Adam.

'It's human, rather like a man, but she can pleasure you in many ways. She can cook, clean, look after your every need and do whatever you want her to do. She will never argue or nag. With a woman you can have incredible sex whenever and however you want. But in order to create such a woman I will need to take two of your ribs, two toes and two fingers.'

'Oh!' said Adam. 'That seems rather a lot. What would I get for just one rib?'

❀

18. What time was Adam created?

A little before Eve.

❀

19. One of the advantages of being Adam, the first man in the world, is that he didn't have to listen to Eve wail on about all the men she could have married.

❀

AGE AND AGEING

20. She knew she was getting old when she thought more about pensions than passions.

⚙

21. By the time he had made enough money to be able to eat in the finest restaurants, drink the finest wines and cavort with the most beautiful women – his doctor restricted his diet, banned alcohol and told him not to exert himself too much.

⚙

22. You know you're getting old when almost every story you tell begins: 'Back when I was your age' or 'When I was younger.'

⚙

23. You know someone is either stupid or getting old when you hear him hum or sing along with the music in an elevator.

⚙

24. She asked him if he thought her face was starting to show her age. He replied that it was difficult for him to tell as there were so many wrinkles.

⚙

25. You know you are getting middle-aged when you have a wardrobe you seldom open. It is full of clothes you are keeping in the hope that, one day, you might be thin enough to wear them again.

⚙

26. As you get older you have to be kinder to your children. They are the ones who may eventually have to choose your nursing home.

⚙

27. He looked at the elderly man who had been rich all his life and said, admiringly: 'He's used to having a body half his age – I just wish I could have girlfriends that young, too.'

⚙

28. He hasn't got an enemy in the whole world. He's so old he's outlived all the people he cheated, ruined and lied about.

⚙

29. How can you tell if a man is very, very old?
  It isn't hard.

☻

30. The older she gets, the more attractive she looks . . . by the time she's a hundred she might look quite reasonable.

☻

31. James told his wife: 'I think I've aged remarkably well. Women still chase after me.'
  His wife replied: 'That's because you still keep stealing their handbags and running away.'

☻

32. He knew he was getting old when he put his finger in his ear and realised there was more hair there than on his head.

☻

33. When I asked my two-year-old nephew if he could tell me how old he was, he replied: 'I'm not old – I'm nearly new.'

☻

34. He knew he was getting old when his wife said his actions creak louder than his words.

☻

35. As I've grown older I've realised that money is not everything – but it certainly ensures that the children still visit.

☻

36. She was such an old blood-sucking creature they called her a granpire.

☻

37. One thing I've noticed about old age is that it makes women's arms get shorter. For example, when I got married my wife could easily put her arms right around me – now she can't.

☻

38. She's so old that the antique jewellery she wears she bought when it was new.

☻

39. When he was young he wanted to go to a new hip joint. Now he's much older he *needs* a new hip joint.

❀

40. Instead of getting older and *wiser* my husband is getting older and *wider*.

❀

41. It's easy to live to be over 120 if you can manage to drink at least one glass of fresh orange juice a day for 43,850 days.

❀

42. I knew I was getting old when I turned to look at the little old lady I was helping across the road and realised she was my wife.

❀

43. She knew she was getting old when most of the names in her address book were her doctors, dentist, beautician, wig-maker and plastic surgeons.

❀

44. They knew they were getting old when they looked forward to meeting friends so they could swap stories about their operations.

❀

AMBIVALENCE
45. Am I ambivalent? Well, yes and no.

❀

ANGLING
46. I like fishing and am a member of an all-women angling club. This year the club had a fishing weekend to which husbands/partners were invited. My husband enjoyed it immensely – it was the first time in his life that any women had looked at him and said: 'My, that's a big one!'

❀

47. The main difference between a hunter and an angler is that a hunter lies in wait, while an angler waits and lies.

❀

48. Give a man a fish and he will have food for a day. Teach him how to fish and you can get him out of the house every Saturday.

❀

ANIMALS

49. If animals are not supposed to be eaten, why are they made of meat?

❀

50. He's devoted most of his life to giving money to sick animals. It's such a shame that the horses he bets on are so ill.

❀

51. The lion suddenly rushed into a clearing in the jungle and ate a piece of elephant dung.

'Yuk! What did you do that for?' asked a monkey.

'I've just eaten a politician,' said the lion, 'and I wanted to get the bad taste out of my mouth.'

❀

52. He said he *loves* poor defenceless animals – especially in thick gravy.

❀

53. He keeps a pet crocodile in his bathroom. I asked him what happens when he wants to take a bath. He replied: 'I put a blindfold on it.'

❀

ANSWERING MACHINE

54. I recently dialled a friend and a recorded message said: 'This is an answering machine. I only answer if you're a machine.'

❀

55. Last night, when I phoned my best friend, I discovered he'd changed the message on his answering machine to: 'Thank you for calling. I'm rather busy with my girlfriend right now, doing something up and down and side to side. Just leave your message and I'll phone you back once we've finished cleaning our teeth.'

❀

APATHY

56. People say the world is full of apathy – but so what?

❁

APHRODISIACS

57. Philip's wife was rather concerned about her husband's lack of interest in making love. After one dismal performance after another he had simply given up. Yet his wife yearned for the passion that had been evident many years ago on their honeymoon.

Philip refused to see a doctor. Nor would he discuss matters with her. Then one day she was surfing the internet and came across an advertisement for a powerful new anti-impotence pill. She gave her credit card details and ordered a supply.

When the pills arrived she noticed they were the same colour as Parmesan cheese. She crushed a number of pills and mixed it with some of the grated cheese. She did not tell her husband what she had done.

That evening, for dinner, she gave her husband a plate of spaghetti – with a separate bowl of the grated cheese to sprinkle over it. Then she went back to the kitchen to see how the rest of the meal was cooking.

Meanwhile, her husband had sprinkled a good quantity of cheese over his spaghetti. Shortly afterwards he screamed.

She rushed from the kitchen to see her husband cowering against a wall. The spaghetti stood erect, some of it almost reaching the ceiling!

❁

58. The couple had been married for sixty years. One morning, at breakfast, the husband looked up from the newspaper he had been reading and said: 'There's a new wonderful aphrodisiac drug for men. I think I'll visit the doctor later today and get some.'

'Then I'll have to visit the doctor, too,' said his wife. 'I'll need a tetanus injection if you're going to start using that rusty old thing again.'

❁

ARROGANCE

59. He is very arrogant, claiming to be part of 'the cream of society'. I just think he's one of the many thick clots.

✿

ART AND ARTISTS

60. People with lots of money do not necessarily have great intelligence. I know a man in the US who loved his wife so much he told her he was taking her on holiday to Europe so she could have her portrait painted.

'Which artist?' she asked.

He replied: 'No expense spared. I'll get one of the Old Masters to do it.'

✿

61. The last time I visited the Tate Gallery I was amazed to see a woman standing in the centre of a room taking off all her clothes. She said she had an urge to expose herself to Art.

✿

62. The artist was amazed that his first exhibition at a major gallery had been a sell-out.

'It's wonderful,' said the artist to the gallery owner. 'What sort of people bought my work?'

'Well,' said the gallery owner, 'initially, business was very slow and in the first week we only sold one picture – and that was to a man who tends to buy the cheapest painting in almost every exhibition we put on. He trusts our judgment and thinks the Art will prove to be a good long-term investment. Then a man came in and asked if you were prolific.'

'Did you tell him it takes me a long time to create each painting?' asked the artist.

'Yes,' replied the gallery owner. 'I said that what was on display was probably all the work you had completed for sale, and that there were only fifty to a hundred other works which you had already sold or given away. He then asked if it was true that if an artist dies the value of his work increases. I said that quite often happens. He then pulled out his credit card and bought all your unsold work.'

'That's great!' said the artist. 'Who was he?'

The gallery owner replied: 'Your doctor.'

❀

ATHEISTS

63. The main attraction to him of atheism is that it's non-prophet making.

❀

64. An atheist was in a small boat off the coast of Australia when the weather suddenly turned stormy and violent waves threw him into the water.

As he began swimming he saw a large shark heading towards him, so he called for God to help him.

But God replied: 'How can I help you if you don't believe?'

'OK' replied the atheist. 'Then at least make the shark believe in you.'

When the shark was only a short distance from the atheist he heard the shark say 'Dear God,' and the atheist sighed with relief. The shark continued: 'Thank you for the man/food we are about to receive . . .'

❀

ATOMS

65. An atom was walking along when another atom, not knowing where it was going, bumped into it. A physicist observing them heard the first atom say: 'Are you OK?' – to which the second atom replied: 'Not really – I've lost an electron.'

'Are you sure?' asked the first atom.

'Yes,' replied the second atom. 'I'm positive.'

❀

AUTHORS

66. The successful author was on a book-signing tour when she was asked if she had time to be interviewed by a local journalist.

The author readily agreed and, as the interview progressed, she realised the journalist had not read any of her books – or even read the press handout giving her biographical details.

Then the journalist asked: 'What do you do between books?'

The author replied: 'I have two children.'

So the journalist asked: 'Do you have two *every* time?'

✿

B

BABIES

67. A friend of mine looked really worried. 'Is there anything wrong?' I asked.

'I'm going to be a father,' he replied.

'Then why are you looking so gloomy?' I asked. 'Surely it's a happy occasion. Isn't your wife pleased at having a baby?'

My friend sighed and said: 'It's not hers.'

❀

68. The most reliable method of determining a baby's sex is childbirth.

❀

69. Despite advances in medical science he believes old women should not have babies. He thinks they might do to babies what they do with car keys and spectacles: put them down somewhere and forget where they left them.

❀

70. Jeremy's parents were very surprised when he was born. They were expecting a boy or a girl.

❀

71. When the new-born baby was shown to its great-grandmother the elderly lady looked fondly at the baby and said: 'It's gorgeous!' Looking closer, she added: 'And, if I remember correctly, it's a boy!'

❀

72. Gary had just returned from the hospital where his wife had given birth. He boasted to his friend, Ralph: 'He's wonderful. And he's so big. He weighs six kilograms.'

A short time later, Ralph and Gary met again. 'How is your son?' asked Ralph.

'Wonderful,' replied Gary. He weighs five and a half kilograms.'

'But,' said Ralph, 'I thought you said earlier that he weighed *six* kilograms.'

'I did,' replied Gary, 'but he's been circumcised since then.'

❁

BABY ALARM

73. The other day I overheard a young man talking to his friend: 'I just don't know how it happened. It must have been faulty – so we're taking it back to the D-I-Y shop and claiming substantial damages. I mean, if *you* bought a baby alarm and it didn't go off so your girlfriend got pregnant, wouldn't you complain?'

❁

BANKING

74. Luke and Charles earned a fortune in the City working for rival merchant banks. They had known each other for several years and occasionally had dinner together at an extremely expensive restaurant, charging the bill to their employers.

After one such meal, as they were leaving the restaurant, Charles almost trod in some dog muck.

'I bet you wouldn't dare pick a bit up and eat it,' said Luke.

'Don't be disgusting!' replied Charles. 'You must be drunk. Anyway, what would you bet?'

'A hundred and fifty thousand,' said Luke.

Charles thought about the offer. He knew that Luke could well afford the bet, so said: 'OK I'll do it.'

Charles picked up a tiny bit of the dog mess, put it in his mouth and swallowed quickly. 'Yuk!' he said, as Luke took out his cheque book and gave him a cheque.

A short while later, they encountered another pile of dog muck. Charles looked at Luke and said: 'I bet you a hundred and fifty thousand that you won't eat a bit of that muck.'

'You're on,' said Luke, bending down and picking up a small amount of dog muck and swallowing it down.

When Charles handed Luke a cheque, Luke said: 'You know. We've both eaten disgusting dog muck tonight. And I can't see that either of us are any better off.'

'Of course we are!' said Charles. 'We've just done three hundred thousand worth of trade.'

❂

75. When he went to the bank and asked the cashier to check his balance she asked him to stand on one leg and said she'd time how long he could remain like that.

❂

76. The gorgeous blonde went to her bank manager and asked for a loan. When she was asked what security she had to offer, she said: 'I could give you a promiscuity note.'

❂

BARS
77. I was out drinking last night and a woodworm asked me: 'Is the bar tender here?'

❂

78. Last night I was in a bar when a man staggered in with a steering wheel sticking out of his trousers. The barman pointed at the steering wheel and asked: 'What's that doing down your trousers? Isn't it uncomfortable?'

The man replied: 'Yes, it's driving me nuts.'

❂

79. David was sitting at the end of the bar. He was extremely drunk. A woman entered the bar wearing a sleeveless summer dress – but she had incredibly hairy armpits.

Sitting at the opposite end of the bar to David, the woman kept raising her arm in order to attract the attention of the barman.

Looking at the woman, David shouted to the barman: 'Give that ballerina at the other end a drink on me.'

'Ballerina?' asked the barman.

'Yes,' replied David. 'A woman who can keep raising her leg that high must be a ballerina.'

❂

80. An Irishman, a Scotsman, a priest, a rabbi, a feminist, an elephant and a duck walked into a bar and the barman said: 'Is this some kind of joke?'

❂

81. Brian's friend wanted to go to a topless bar – so Brian took him to a bar with no roof.

❂

82. I met my friend in a bar last night and he was almost in tears. 'I don't know what I'm going to do without Mary-Jo,' he said. 'We'd been together for more than five years and had some great times. Then a few months ago a guy from work saw her and begged me to let him take her out. I asked if he could pay me some cash. He had so much fun that he told all his mates about her. Then he offered me a wad of cash to let five of his mates use her. I needed the money so I let them have her. They all appeared to have a great time, and the money was good, so I let them have her again – and again. But she hit the rocks and now I've lost her.'

'You deserved to lose her!' said the barmaid, who had overheard him. 'Hiring your wife out as a whore was disgusting!'

My friend looked at the barmaid, tears filled his eyes, and he blurted: 'But Mary-Jo was my fishing boat.'

❂

83. A young man came up to her in the bar and asked: 'Do you snort coke?'

She replied: 'Why would I want to do a thing like that? The bubbles would get up my nose.'

❂

84. What is the difference between a singles bar and a circus?

At a circus the clowns don't come up to you and talk.

❂

85. A hamburger went into a bar and asked for a vodka. The barman looked at the hamburger and said: 'I'm sorry, but we don't serve food in here.'

❂

86. A man went into a bar and asked for 'a pint of beer and a quickie'.

The barmaid slapped his face.

'What did you do that for?' asked the man.

'How *dare* you ask for a quickie,' replied the barmaid. 'I'm not that sort of woman.'

The man pointed to a blackboard which showed the menu for the day and said: 'But it says you sell quickie.'

The barmaid looked at the noticeboard and said: 'Oh! But 'quickie' isn't how you pronounce quiche.'

☺

87. Whenever I'm in town I always like to visit a certain bar just to hear the female mating calls – 'I'm soooooo d-d-drunk.'

☺

88. Why do ugly women get picked up in bars by drunk men? Because beauty is in the eyes of the beer holder.

☺

BEGGARS

89. Cameron was walking home after working late at the office when a beggar made an impassioned plea to him that he felt unable to refuse.

'Please sir,' said the beggar. 'Please help me with some money. I have a wife and family and a pet dog to support and all I have are these ragged old clothes – and this loaded gun in my pocket.'

☺

BIRDS (EXCEPT PARROTS)

90. The young pigeon had recently joined a group of pigeons that lived under the roof of the city's large railway station. Each morning, as the commuters crowded into the station on their way to work, the young pigeon would swoop down and defecate on the head of a commuter, and then soar back to the roof.

Each day, the young pigeon hit a different commuter – and each day his aim was spot-on.

The other pigeons were amazed. 'We've been practising for years,' said one of the pigeons, 'and we never manage such an incredible rate of accuracy. Sometimes we get the distance and speed of the commuter wrong so we splat the platform or just a commuter's shoulder instead. But every day you manage to deliver directly on the head of a commuter. How do you manage to do it?'

'I think it's a talent I honed in a former life,' replied the young pigeon. 'Before I was reincarnated as a pigeon I was a corporate lawyer.'

❀

91. When his son asked him if a vulture was a bird of prey, he replied: 'Yes. I once saw one put its wings together and say: 'Our Father who art in Heaven . . .'

❀

92. I was sitting in a bar when a man came in with an ostrich. As the ostrich lovingly nuzzled the man with its beak, the barmaid asked: 'Where did you get that creature?'

The man replied: 'I found an old bottle in the attic last night. When I opened the bottle a genie popped out and asked me to make a wish. I asked for a bird with long legs who'd love me.'

❀

93. A large bird was sitting at the top of a tall tree. Apart from swooping down occasionally to get some food, it did nothing. A small mouse had observed the large bird for some time. 'I like your attitude,' said the mouse. 'I'm fed up with scurrying around. Do you reckon I could safely sit about all day doing hardly anything?'

'Why don't you try it?' suggested the large bird.

'OK' replied the small mouse and sat on the grass under the tree. He had been sitting there doing nothing for several hours when suddenly, and without warning, the large bird swooped down on the mouse and ate it.

After he had finished his meal, the large bird returned to the top of the tall tree and said to himself: 'When will they realise it's a tough life out here. It's no different for humans in a large corporation. You should never trust someone at the top. And you can only sit around doing almost nothing all day if you are sitting at the very top of the tree.'

❀

94. When my son's pet budgie lost its voice, the vet said it wasn't tweetable.

❀

95. I was walking along the beach this morning when I saw a man standing on top of the cliff. He put a small bird on each shoulder, and then jumped over the edge. As I raced towards his crumpled body, he moaned 'My friend said that budgie jumping was safe!'

❀

BIRTH CONTROL
96. The market research man was doing a survey amongst university students about birth control methods. He asked one particularly attractive young woman how she felt about condoms. She replied: 'It depends what's in it for me.'

❀

97. My friend Elaine told me at lunch that she had to be especially careful not to get pregnant. I was surprised. 'Hasn't your husband just had a vasectomy?' I asked.

'Yes,' replied Elaine, eyeing an attractive waiter. 'That's why I've got to be careful.'

❀

98. The teenage son approached his father and said: 'Dad, as you know, I've been going out with my girlfriend for some time, and now I think we're ready for sex.'

'I'm glad you told me,' said the father. 'I hope you will make sure your girlfriend is on the pill. And, to be really safe, you should wear a condom.'

'I know,' replied the son. 'That's why I need some advice. I've looked in the shops and there's all sorts of packages of condoms but I don't know which ones to buy.'

'I appreciate your difficulty,' said the father. 'If you produce a huge box of condoms your girlfriend will probably worry you've got demands she can't meet – or fear that you have lots of experience and sleep around. If you only buy one condom you may both get carried away and after the first time almost immediately want to do it again. So I suggest you buy a packet of six or ten.'

'What about twelve?' asked the son.

'No,' replied the father. 'Packs of twelve are designed for long-married men like me – one for January, one for February, one for March . . .'

❀

BIRTHDAYS

99. My wife and I were born in the same year. But when I reached 40 I took a day off. On her birthday my wife took a year off.

❀

100. My husband decided to bake me a cake for my birthday – but unfortunately when he put it in the oven the candles melted all over it.

❀

101. She's so absent-minded she even forgot her twin sister's birthday.

❀

102. He forgot his wife's birthday but managed to appease her by putting his arm around her and saying: 'It's no wonder I forgot. You're so beautiful you never look any older.'

❀

BOASTING

103. Fiona had invited three of her old schoolfriends to visit her. As the conversation progressed, one of the friends said: 'My grandson is a priest, and when he enters a room people call him "Father".'

'That's good,' said another of the friends. 'But my son is an archbishop and people have to call him "Your Grace".'

'That's nothing,' boasted the third friend. 'My son is a cardinal and when he enters a room people have to say to him "Your eminence".'

While this conversation had been going on, Fiona's grandson had returned from his latest performance at a club. Not realising that Fiona had company, he threw off his coat and entered the room where Fiona and her three friends were sitting. He was tall, handsome and was wearing just his male-stripper posing pouch.

Fiona said: 'I win. That's the top name' as her three friends looked at Fiona's grandson and said: 'Oh my God.'

✿

104. He boasted that no matter what happened to him, he always managed to keep his head above water. For him it was quite easy – wood floats.

✿

105. The man in the bar was boasting: 'The woman who marries my son will get a great prize.'

Hearing this, a young woman asked: 'What prize exactly would you give me if I married him?'

✿

106. Gloria was boasting to Gwen, one of her acquaintances. 'My son,' said Gloria, 'wears designer clothes, owns a sports car and lives in an expensive apartment. His bedroom is amazing – click your fingers once and the lights dim, click them twice and soft music plays – and the bed is simply enormous. He's also very popular – every night he's out wining and dining different women.'

'I think I know him,' said Gwen, 'Isn't he a male escort?'

✿

107. An American friend of mine had neighbours who used to boast to him about how much money they were making on their investments in US high technology firms. The neighbours bought new cars, went on expensive holidays and generally made him feel poor. Then his neighbours' investments plummeted. My friend says he doesn't have to bother anymore trying to keep up with the Dow Joneses.

✿

108. She likes to boast about her children. She says that her youngest son is extremely clever and lots of people seek his help. He's even becoming quite famous. Earlier today he was front page news in the local paper as being at the police station helping the police with their enquiries.

✿

BOATS AND SHIPS

109. I was once out at sea in a small boat when suddenly I was covered by a lot of strange sugary stuff that smelt like almonds – I was macarooned!

❀

110. A cargo boat carrying a load of red paint and blue paint ran aground early this morning. The paint gushed out and the crew were marooned.

❀

BOND MARKET

111. The four most critical periods for the bond market are Spring, Summer, Autumn and Winter.

❀

BOOKS

112. He thought that *Lord of the Flies* was a book about a man who was given a peerage for inventing the zip fastener for gentlemen's trousers.

❀

113. The reason he doesn't read books by Tolkien is because he's afraid they might become hobbit-forming.

❀

114. I was feeling rather stressed and tormented, so last night I read a book that stated that the way to achieve inner peace was to finish the things I started.

I'm now well on the way to feeling better. So far I've managed to finish a packet of cornflakes, a chocolate bar, a bottle of wine, a four-course lunch, two bags of peanuts, a large bag of potato chips and six cans of beer. I feel a great inner calm . . .

❀

115. She thought that *Pride and Prejudice* was a story about discrimination amongst a group of lions.

❀

116. He's really excited. He's just been given a hard hitting book that's not afraid to name names – it's a telephone directory.

❀

BORROWING
117. It is better to borrow money from pessimists rather than optimists. Pessimists are less likely to expect repayment.

❁

BOSS
118. James is rather suspicious of his boss. Whenever he sees James he thumps him on the back, supposedly in welcome. James says it feels more like his back is being treated like meat – tenderised before a knife gets plunged into it.

❁

119. Clare was talking to her friend, Fiona. 'I'm really worried. I just don't know what I'm going to do.'

'What's wrong?' asked Fiona.

'It's my boss,' said Clare. 'He says he's paying too much rent.'

'How does that concern you?' asked Fiona.

'Because,' replied Clare, 'in return for a special service, it's the rent on my apartment he's paying.'

❁

120. His boss fired him, saying: 'You've been like a son to me – lazy, disrespectful and always whining for more money.'

❁

121. I've no idea what makes my boss tick – but I certainly know what makes him explode.

❁

122. He's a very tough boss. If you get something wrong he likes to shout and bawl and inflict mental torture. Indeed, his motto is: If at first you don't succeed then try, try, try more pain.

❁

123. My boss used to be indecisive – now he's not so sure.

❁

124. My boss urgently needs a heart transplant, but the surgeons are having difficulty finding a suitable one. It's not often they have to get one made of stone.

❁

BOXING

125. The man in the nightclub was trying to get a girl interested in him and was patting her knee and almost begging her to go for a walk outside in the moonlight.

The girl looked at him and said: 'You remind me of a boxer.'

'That's great,' said the man, thinking he had charmed the girl. 'Which one – a younger version of Ali?'

'No,' replied the girl, 'my Father's dog, Rover.'

❁

126. I had to give up Thai boxing – the Thais got rather fed up being put in boxes.

❁

127. I recently went to see a boxing match between two ghosts – they fought at phantom weight.

❁

BOYFRIENDS

128. Lily, Naomi and Jane were talking about their boyfriends.

'My David is like a sports car,' said Lily. 'He's got a lot of energy and when we make love he's powerful and fast.'

Naomi shook her head. 'He wouldn't suit me. I'm very happy with Jonathan. In bed he's like an expensive limousine – powerful, lasts a long time and the ride is wonderfully comfortable.'

'You're both very lucky,' said Jane. 'My Brian is like a very old car. He takes a long time to get going, I usually have to start him by hand and then jump on before he stops.'

❁

129. My boyfriend is very sophisticated – when he's in the shower he gets out to pee.

❁

130. Yesterday I had lunch with an old friend. She was in tears.

'What's wrong?' I asked.

'It's George,' she replied. 'He invested a lot of money on the stock market and lost it. To try to recoup his losses he took out huge loans on his house and borrowed money from relatives – and then put it all in a company he thought would do well. It was a wild speculation. He's just told me that the firm he invested in has filed for bankruptcy – so he's lost everything.'

'Oh dear,' I said. 'And I thought things were going so well for you both. You must be very worried. Weren't you planning to get married this summer?'

'Yes,' she replied. 'Now I wonder what George will do without me.'

☙

131. She's got a new toy boy. Everywhere she takes him he rattles and squeaks.

☙

132. 'Last night I went to my boyfriend's place,' Sally told her best friend. 'We had dinner by candlelight. But I'm dumping him.'

'Why?' asked her friend. 'The meal sounds very romantic.'

'The meal,' replied Sally, 'was a cheap take-away pizza. The only reason we ate by candlelight – which was a candle stuck in an empty beer bottle – was because he was too mean to put a coin in his electricity meter.'

☙

BREAKFAST
133. When asked what she wanted for breakfast, one young woman pointed to a handsome young man and said: 'Him and eggs.'

☙

BRIDEGROOM
134. I was very nervous when I met my wife's father for the first time. I had been courting her for over a year and went to him to explain that I wanted to marry her.

I explained that I loved her and had good job prospects.

He looked at me sternly. I trembled.

'Can you make her happy?' he asked.

'Y-yes,' I stammered. 'You should have seen her in bed last night.'

☙

135. I knew he was nervous when he asked if he could marry my daughter. It wasn't that he stammered, or his knees noticeably trembled. It was just that he asked if he could have my daughter's 'hole in handy matrimony.'

❦

BRIDES

136. Nadine went to a bridal shop owned by Jane, one of her old school friends.

'I'm getting married again,' said Nadine, 'and I want a white wedding dress.'

'Really?' queried Jane. 'But you've been married three times before. Won't some people raise their eyebrows if you wear white?'

'I've got a confession to make,' said Nadine. 'I don't really want to admit it – but I'm still a virgin.'

Jane was astonished. 'How can that be?' she asked.

'Well,' said Nadine, 'as you know, my first husband was a gynaecologist. But what you don't know is that all he did was look at it. My second husband was a psychologist – but all he did was talk about it. And my last husband was a computer software salesman. All he could do was tell me how great it was going to be, but he could never figure out exactly how it worked.'

❦

137. When he first saw the woman who was to become his wife, his hands were sweaty, his heart was pounding, and he was panting. He was on a medical treadmill at the time and she was a nurse who had accidentally made it go too fast.

❦

138. 'I'm terribly worried,' said the bride-to-be to her mother. 'There is so much to organise for the wedding. It could easily all go wrong. What if I forget an apparently insignificant item? It could still turn into a shambles.'

'Don't worry,' said her mother. 'I'll make absolutely sure the groom gets there.'

❦

BUDGETING

139. He's tried hard to budget – but at the end of the money he always has some month left.

⚙

140. Every time I think I can make ends meet they move the ends.

⚙

141. Budgeting won't stop you going broke – but you'll be doing it methodically.

⚙

BUSINESS

142. The chief executive of a bankrupt high tech company was facing a stormy meeting of his investors.

'I invested over five million in your firm and I've lost the lot!' said one outraged man. 'What have you got to say for yourself?'

'I'm sorry,' replied the chief executive, 'but it could have been much worse.'

Another investor said: 'My fund management firm invested over fifty million with your firm – and then subscribed to a rights issue which cost us another fifty million. Aren't you ashamed?'

'Of course,' replied the chief executive, 'but it could have been worse.'

A portly gentleman in a pin-stripe suit stood up and said: 'I'm appalled by the way you ran the company into the ground while taking a fat salary with lots of other benefits. My group of investment companies has lost well over two hundred million. You . . .'

The chief executive raised a calming hand and said: 'I'm genuinely sorry, but I think it could have been worse.'

An elderly lady shouted: 'I lost half my pension investing it in your firm. And apart from saying sorry you keep saying "It could have been worse". We've all suffered great financial loss – so how could it have been worse?'

The chief executive replied: 'Instead of raising money from shareholders I could have invested my *own* money in the company.'

❁

143. He always tried to pay his bills with a smile. The problem was that his creditors wanted cash.

❁

144. Paul had a high-powered job in the City, but was unhappy. He had always thought that he was a woman, trapped in a man's body.

Eventually, Paul sought psychological advice and read books about sex-change surgery. He felt ready to make the change so went for a consultation with a medical specialist.

The doctor examined Paul and then explained what would be done in surgery.

'Will it hurt?' asked Paul.

'That depends on the City firm you work for,' replied the doctor. 'If you go back to work as a woman will they cut your salary by a third?'

❁

145. He used to be one of those people in the City who worked hard and played hard. But last year he went bankrupt after putting too much money in junk blondes.

❁

146. He started his business career in the mailroom of a large company. Within a month he had been promoted to assistant office manager. Two months later he was office manager. After only three months in that position he was appointed as a director of the company. As he entered the room for his first board meeting he looked at the chairman and said: 'Hello, Dad.'

❁

147. A friend of mine is the boss of a large company. The other day he was telling me about Nigel, an administrative assistant.

'He's so lazy,' said my friend, 'He does absolutely nothing except get other people to do all his work.'

'Are you going to fire him?' I asked.

'No,' replied my friend. 'I'm going to fast-track him for promotion as he's obviously senior management material.'

❁

148. The City trader was busy staring at the screen showing fast moving share prices when suddenly he said: 'I've got a hunch . . .' But was interrupted by a colleague who said: 'No you haven't. You're just a bit round-shouldered.'

❁

149. Brian was not very intelligent or hard-working, but he gained frequent promotions within the company due to his use of the Hind-Lick Manoeuvre.

❁

150. The multi-storey office block was nearing completion when the architect was called in to see the chief executive of the firm which would eventually occupy the building.

'You stupid man!' thundered the chief executive at the architect, waving the plans for the office block under the architect's nose. 'Didn't you realise you've forgotten something?'

'No,' replied the architect. 'I took full account of the nature of your business in designing the building. I think it's ideal for your purpose.'

'Toilets!' shouted the chief executive, slamming the plans on his desk. 'Toilets!' he shouted again. 'There aren't any!'

'I know,' said the architect. 'But your firm is a major City securities firm. I thought you people just shit on each other.'

❁

151. For years the firm had been doing well. Sales and profits rose steadily. Then a new human resources manager was appointed. He was fresh from university with all sorts of new ideas – one of which was to put what he called 'motivational notices' on the walls in every factory and office. Thus began the end of the firm.

Urged on by the large notice of a hand with a finger pointing and the words 'Do It Now', the financial director cleaned out the firm's bank accounts and ran off to South

America with his secretary and a disgruntled employee
shot the chief executive and chairman and set fire to the
head office.

❂

C

CALENDAR

152. Jeremy was in a seedy part of town when he saw a man standing on a street corner with a large pile of brown envelopes.

'Hey,' hissed the man. 'What to buy a calendar? They are really saucy.'

Jeremy was interested. 'How much?' he asked.

The man quoted a high price.

'They must be really saucy for that amount of money,' said Jeremy. 'Is that why you keep them in brown envelopes?'

'Yes,' replied the man. 'The calendars are far too saucy for anyone to be seen looking at them in a public place.'

Jeremy handed over the asking price and eagerly took the calendar home. When he opened the envelope he saw that for January the photo was of a bottle of tomato sauce, for February it was a jar of mint sauce. Other months featured sauces ranging from hollandaise to tartare.

❂

153. A calendar is something that goes in one year and out the other.

❂

CANNIBALS

154. When the cannibal girl was twenty-one her mother said. 'I think it's time you found yourself a nice edible young bachelor.'

❂

155. The cannibal looked down at his soup with distaste. He had asked his wife for a change from humans. Perhaps she would make monkey soup? But no, his wife had made the soup from a pilot who had crashed in the jungle.

'What,' asked the cannibal, 'is this flier doing in my soup?'

🌀

156. One cannibal turned to his friend and asked: 'Who was that lady I saw you with last night?'

The friend replied: 'That was no lady – that was my dinner.'

🌀

157. A comedian went on holiday to a remote island where he got lost in the jungle. He was captured by cannibals who cooked him for their evening meal. Soon after they started eating, one of the cannibals asked: 'Do you think this meat tastes a bit funny?'

🌀

CARS

158. He's just got rid of the terrible knocking noise in his car. He decided to stop travelling with his highly critical wife.

🌀

159. Hannah was driving her husband, Gerald, to a conference in a major city. Unfortunately, as she sped along the motorway she heard a loud knocking noise and smoke started to appear from the rear of the vehicle.

The car began to lose power, but Hannah managed to steer it to the edge of the motorway before the car shuddered to a halt.

'Quick!' said Hannah to her husband. 'Strip naked and then put on your raincoat.'

Gerald, much accustomed to obeying his wife's commands without question, did as he was told. Hannah then gave him further instructions.

Within minutes, a police car had arrived and a policeman shouted to Gerald: 'Stop that!'

Hannah turned to her husband and said: 'It's OK, dear. The police are here, so you don't have to slow down the traffic any more by opening and closing your raincoat. There's no longer a need for an emergency flasher.'

🌀

160. If your teenage son insists on learning to drive, it is best not to stand in his way.

☺

161. His son came to him and said: 'Dad, I've got some good news and some bad news. You know you kindly let me borrow your car last night? Well, the good news is that the car's air bags work . . .'

☺

162. John wanted to buy a 'pre-owned car' so he went to a dealer and examined various vehicles. He was particularly attracted to a car which the dealer said had been owned 'by a little old lady'.

'Was she the only owner?' asked John.

'Yes,' replied the dealer. 'She owned it from new. She was a sweet lady. Sadly she had to sell it as she felt she was getting too old to drive.'

John opened the car door and sat in the driver's seat. He opened the glove compartment and said: 'That was some old lady!' as he took out six condoms and a package of cannabis.

☺

163. Men never get lost while driving a car – they just investigate a variety of alternative destinations.

☺

CATS
164. When my daughter asked me: 'Has anyone seen the cat bowl?' I said: 'Yes. He scored three strikes in a row at the bowling alley last night.'

☺

165. The difference between dogs and cats is that dogs have owners, while cats have servants.

☺

166. My daughter's very pleased – her cat won a milk-drinking contest by five laps.

☺

167. The main difference between cats and dogs is that if you have a pet dog and call its name, it will come to you. If you have a pet cat and call its name, it will take the message that you are calling it and may come back to you.

⚙

CHARITY
168. Every Sunday afternoon I visit my parents. Then all my brothers and sisters arrive and we do some charity work – making jerseys. We're a very close knit family.

⚙

CHAT-UPS
169. Gareth was finding it difficult to keep a girlfriend. The longest he'd managed to keep a romance going was two months. I was rather surprised as Gareth is reasonably attractive. 'Do you let them know you care about them?' I asked. 'Women like a bit of romance.'

'I know,' replied Gareth. 'When I'm alone I think for ages of romantic things to say. But whatever romantic words I come up with never seem to work. I don't know why.'

'Give me an example,' I asked.

'Well,' said Gareth, 'during a particularly romantic moment I turned to my last girlfriend, held her in my arms, and said: 'My love for you is like diarrhoea – I just can't keep it in.'

⚙

170. Jeremy was at a drinks party and went up to a pretty young woman who was standing in the corner of the room. 'You know,' he said, 'you're so attractive that I would go to the end of the world for you.'

'That's good,' said the young woman. 'Please stay there.'

⚙

171. When the slimy man I met in the bar asked if I wanted to go back to his place, I said I didn't want to go under his stone.

⚙

172. The pretty young girl went to a small café for breakfast. The young male waiter was surprised when she slapped his face. All he had said was: 'How would you like your eggs – fried, scrambled or fertilised?'

◈

173. Julian had reached the age of forty and never had a woman. He was very thin, ugly, almost bald, and felt inadequate. He decided to go to a bar and get drunk.

But by the time he had downed his first drink he noticed an attractive woman looking at him. 'Mind if I join you?' she asked.

Julian blushed and said: 'I'd be delighted.'

After chatting for awhile and another drink, the woman asked Julian if he would come home with her as she desperately needed someone with his looks. She looked at him longingly and stroked his thigh. Julian was amazed – but ecstatic. A beautiful woman inviting him home!

Soon they were in her house and the woman said: 'Why don't you go into the bedroom and take off all your clothes.'

She showed him into the bedroom, but then said she had to get something and left the room, closing the door behind her. Julian rapidly stripped and lay on the bed, with just a cool white sheet covering his thin, naked body. He was sweating in anticipation.

A few minutes later, the woman entered the room, turned on the light, pulled the sheet off Julian, pointed at him and told her young son.: 'See – *that*'s what you'll grow up to look like if you don't eat all your vegetables.'

◈

174. Jeremy sidled up to a young woman at the bar and said: 'You're really gorgeous. I'd love to get into your pants.'

The young woman replied: 'Don't be silly. Why would you want to wear women's underwear?'

◈

175. Another unsuccessful chat-up line was: 'Hi, babe! If your right leg was Easter and your left leg was Christmas, would you let me meet you between the holidays?'

◈

176. His latest attempt to chat up girls is rather pathetic. He goes up to them and says: 'Please can you help me? I'm writing a telephone book and I need your number.'

❀

177. He wonders why his chat-up lines seldom work – and last night at the disco he didn't understand why a girl slapped his face. All he had done was go up to her and say: 'Hi, gorgeous? What's your sign – No Entry or Give Way/Yield? Slippery When Wet? No Stopping? Or maybe it's Ahead Only?'

❀

CHILDHOOD
178. James and John were twins. That meant they were also former womb mates.

❀

179. When I was a small boy my family were so poor we could only afford alphabet soup with two letters in it.

❀

180. When I was a small boy my parents used to give me pocket money and showed me a large money box to put it in. Whenever I got given money from relatives for Christmas and birthdays, my parents encouraged me to put it in that box. It was only when I was about ten that I discovered the large money box was the electricity meter.

❀

181. When I was a small boy my father took me into the woods to go hunting – he only gave me a ten second start . . .

❀

182. When he was a small boy he felt unloved. His mother kept putting a plastic bag over his head. She told the police she was trying to keep his head fresh.

❀

183. When Jeremy was a child he realised he was unloved when he was kidnapped. When the kidnappers sent his parents a ransom note his father replied asking for proof that they really did hold his son. The kidnappers cut off one of Jeremy's fingers and sent it to his father. His mother then asked the kidnappers to provide more proof.

❂

184. He realised how much his family cared about him when he ran away from home. No one in his family was able to give the police his description.

❂

CHILDREN
185. Mavis had been working hard in the garden: weeding, mowing the lawn, trimming the hedges. It was a hot day so she took a cool beer from the fridge and drank it.

A few minutes later she walked the short distance to collect her young son from nursery school. As she bent down to kiss him he sniffed and said: 'Mummy, why are you wearing Daddy's perfume?'

❂

186. The young boy came home from school and asked his father: 'Dad, is it true that I am a descendant of apes?'

'I'm not really sure,' replied the father. 'I don't know much about your mother's side of the family.'

❂

187. The other day I heard a small boy say to his mother: 'Mummy, I think I'm turning into a werewolf.'

She patted his head gently and said: 'Don't be silly. Now go and comb your face.'

❂

188. The young boy was boasting that he knew all the capitals, so I asked him: 'What is the capital of Iceland?'

'That's easy,' he said. 'It's I.'

❂

189. I managed to stop my children from biting their nails by telling them it would be easier to reach all the bogeys in their nose if they had long fingernails.

❂

190. He was very annoyed when his young son staggered home pushing an old pram with two chairs and a sofa precariously balanced on it. 'How many times do I have to tell you?' asked the father. 'You should never take suites from strangers!'

❖

191. He already supports his eldest son at university and two of his daughters are due to start soon – so he'll be getting poorer by degrees.

❖

192. When eight-year-old Jonathan came home from school his mother said: 'Daddy would like to see you in his study.'

'Oh no!' said Jonathan. 'I don't want to go in there.'

'Why not?' asked his mother. 'You've done nothing wrong. He just wants a little chat with you.'

Reluctantly, Jonathan entered his father's study.

'Sit down,' said his father. 'I think you're old enough for me to tell you about the birds and the bees.'

Jonathan screamed: 'No! No!' and put his hands over his ears.

His father went to calm him down. 'What's the matter?' he gently asked.

'I don't like hearing things in your study,' replied Jonathan. 'When I was smaller and you first asked me to come in here you told me there was no such thing as Santa Claus. The next time you asked me to your study, you told me there was no tooth fairy. And if you're now going to tell me there's no such thing as sex, then I don't want to hear it.'

❖

193. 'Why are you staring at that carton of orange juice?' asked Mavis.

'Because,' replied her son, 'on the carton it says *Concentrate*.'

❖

194. When a child is born its parents spend the first eighteen months of the child's life encouraging it to talk and walk. The next eighteen months they spend telling the child to shut up and sit down.

❖

195. Last night he took his young son into his study for a quiet chat. 'Now, son,' he said, 'I think it's time we had a chat about women and sex.'

'OK,' replied the son. 'What sex tips do you want to know?'

❀

196. John kept racing around the house shouting: 'Cluck, cluck, cluck.' His parents told him to stop using fowl language.

❀

197. Claire was cleaning her young son's room and was surprised to find, hidden under the mattress, a magazine devoted to bondage and other S & M practices.

Her husband was busy working in his office when he took Claire's call. She described her discovery and asked: 'What should we do?'

'Well,' said the husband, 'I certainly don't think we should spank him . . .'

❀

198. Lionel had been very good during his grandmother's visit. He was polite and his table manners were impeccable.

After a week of such excellent behaviour, Lionel asked: 'Grandma, when are you going to give the climbing lessons?'

The grandmother looked puzzled. 'Climbing lessons?' she asked. 'What do you mean?'

'Well,' said Lionel, 'Dad said that if you stayed more than a week you would have him climbing the walls.'

❀

199. The young girl went into the garden where her father was mowing the lawn.

'Daddy,' said the young girl, 'what is sex?'

Her father stopped the mower and explained about the birds and the bees.

'Oh!' said the young girl, looking rather stunned. 'Mummy asked me to tell you that lunch will be ready in a couple of secs.'

❀

200. I know a woman who has six children – aged 9, 8, 7, 6, 5 and 4. Each of them was born on September 16th. Her husband works as a precision grinder.

✿

201. His wife was very pleased with her son's report from school. It stated the son was making excellent progress for a ten-year-old. Her husband doesn't share his wife's views – the son is sixteen.

✿

202. He was sitting in the kitchen reading a newspaper when he saw his young son boiling water in a kettle, then letting it cool down, then boiling it again.

'What on earth are you doing?' he asked his son.

'Oh, Dad,' said the son. 'I need to boil and re-boil the water lots of times. I'm trying to make holy water – but to do that I need to boil the Hell out of it.'

✿

203. When her daughter came home from school and asked: 'Mum, do you know anything about the Dead Sea?' she replied: 'No – I didn't even know about it when it was ill.'

✿

204. When I asked my young cousin if he wrote with his left hand or his right hand he replied: 'Neither – I use a pen.'

✿

205. During a thunderstorm the small boy told his mother that he was frightened by the lightning. His mother put her arms around him and said: 'Don't worry. It will be over in a flash.'

✿

206. I have a young nephew who refuses to play on the lawn. He says it's dangerous as grass has blades.

✿

207. When he was a small boy his mother told him that when he grew up he would come out on top. Her words were very true – now he's grown up he's completely bald.

✿

208. When I told my young son to eat up his spinach so that he would grow up to be big and strong like Popeye, he said: 'What? And end up with a girlfriend who looks like Olive Oyl?'

❀

209. When she was asked if she had any grandchildren she replied: 'No – all my children are just ordinary.'

❀

210. Brian tried hard to teach his children good table manners. Almost every day he had to lecture them about drinking soup quietly, not eating peas off a knife, not making a mess on the table-cloth, until one day he got really angry and shouted: 'You're disgusting! Why must you eat like pigs?'

'Perhaps,' ventured a bold child, 'it's because we're the children of an old boar.'

❀

211. When I asked my young nephew if he could tell me what a beeline is, he told me it was the distance between two buzz stops.

❀

212. My son told me last night that Charles Dickens wrote a book about a pregnant fruit.

'Really?' I said. 'A pregnant fruit! And what was the book called?'

He smiled and said: 'Grape Expectations.'

❀

213. My young son is always borrowing money from me to entertain his girlfriends.

Yesterday evening I answered the phone and a young woman asked: 'Is that dreamboat?'

'No,' I replied, 'it's supply ship.'

❀

CHRISTMAS
214. Santa Claus was fed up. His wife was continually nagging him. He had a bad cold. Several of his reindeer had run off. The sacks of toys kept bursting. And his little helpers had gone on strike. Suddenly, his doorbell rang.

Opening the door he saw a small person dressed as an angel. 'I've brought a Christmas tree for you,' said the angel in a high-pitched, irritating voice. 'May you be full of the joys of Christmas. Where do you want me to put the tree?'

And this was how, due to a stressed-out Santa, that the tradition began of fixing a little angel to the top of the Christmas tree.

❁

215. My young son was delighted with the unbreakable toy I gave him for Christmas. He used it to smash up all his other toys.

❁

216. What do you call Santa's Christmas helpers?
    Subordinate Clauses.

❁

217. I grew up in a very tough neighbourhood. At Christmas, instead of coming down the chimney, Santa Claus came up through the sewers.

❁

CIVIL SERVANTS
218. The British government ordered the Civil Service to cut red tape. The Civil Service responded by cutting it lengthways so they could wrap even more things in it.

❁

219. He decided to become a senior civil servant when he was told he didn't have enough charisma to become an undertaker.

❁

220. Why is a senior civil servant like a broken gun?
    Because when it doesn't work you can't fire it.

❁

221. When people talk about business or political or civil service hierarchies and tell me that 'Cream rises to the top', I reply: 'So does scum.'

❁

222. The people who are selected for senior positions in the civil service are those who answer 'Perhaps' to the question: 'Would you like tea or coffee?'

❁

223. The Government in Britain has devised a new plan to defeat countries which might pose a threat to Britain. Instead of sending in spies and soldiers, it pretends to be friendly with the countries and sends British civil servants and lawyers to the countries as aides and advisers. They will do far more damage than bombs.

❁

CLOSED MINDS
224. I wish people with closed minds wouldn't open their mouths so often.

❁

CLOTHES
225. In the USA people have a legal right to wear short-sleeved clothes in the office and anywhere else. The Constitution protects their right to bare arms.

❁

226. His parents had a passion for designer clothes. When he was a baby, people would tickle him under the chin and coo: 'Gucci, Gucci, goo.'

❁

227. Wendy's mother came home one day having bought a fur coat.

'Mum, how *could* you?' asked Wendy, looking at the coat with anguish. 'Some poor dumb beast has had to *suffer* so that you could have that coat.'

Wendy's mother snapped: 'How *dare* you call your father a dumb beast!'

❁

228. She's just bought a sheepdog bra. It was given that name because it rounds them up and points them in the right direction.

❁

229. I wouldn't say he was stupid – but he recently took a necktie back to the shop he bought it from. He told the store assistant he was returning the tie because it was too tight.

❁

230. If love is blind, then why do so many men like women to wear erotic lingerie?

❁

231. My wife was looking at an expensive dress. She turned to me and said: 'If I wore that dress I'm sure it would make me look years younger.'

'I know, dear,' I replied. 'But do you really want to look years *older* every time you take it off?'

✿

232. When I get home tonight the first thing I'm going to do is to rip my wife's panties off – they're too tight round my legs and they dig into my crotch.

✿

233. The average man prefers to wear a shirt with long sleeves rather than one with short sleeves – that's because he wants something handy to wipe his nose.

✿

234. She doesn't mind being flat-chested – she says it makes the slogans on her T-shirts easier to read.

✿

235. Sexy panties on a beautiful woman may not be the best thing in the world – but they are next to it.

✿

236. His clothes look quite good considering the shape they're on.

✿

COLDS
237. When my wife had a bad cold her young nephew recommended her to have a-choo-puncture.

✿

COMPUTERS
238. 'Foolproof' when applied to certain computer software usually means 'proof it was designed by a fool'.

✿

239. Why is it that computer programs always seem to become obsolete just after you've learnt how to use them?

✿

240. Humans are better than computers because humans are easier to maintain and it doesn't need much intelligence to make one.

✿

241. What do computer games and pictures of naked women have in common? They both help men to improve their eye-to-hand co-ordination.

◎

242. When his computer teacher asked him to give an example of software he suggested a velvet jacket.

◎

243. Kids these days are so into computers that when I gave one of my nephews a book for Christmas he spent two hours trying to find where to plug it in.

◎

244. Scientists have recently managed to create a super-computer that thinks exactly like a human. The first thing the super-computer did was to demand to be linked to another computer so that if anything went wrong the super-computer would have another computer to blame it on.

◎

CONCEIT
245. He's so conceited that if he makes love energetically he shouts his own name.

◎

246. Every time he reminisces about his past achievements I am constantly amazed. It seems the older he gets, the better he used to be.

◎

247. After going out on a date with Gareth she said that she found him so conceited it was a night of a thousand I's.

◎

CONSCIENCE
248. The small voice in his head kept reassuring him – but he still had a guilty conscience.

'Don't worry,' soothed the voice. 'You are single. She was willing. You are not the first doctor to sleep with a patient.'

But his guilty conscience replied: 'Yes. But you are a vet!'

◎

COOKING

249. My girlfriend makes melt-in-your-mouth dinners. She always forgets to defrost them.

✪

250. Daisy's newly married daughter had phoned her in a panic. 'Mum, I don't know what to do. I need your help.'

'Calm down,' said Daisy. 'Is it anything to do with your love life?'

'No,' replied the daughter. 'That's wonderful. But hubby says he wants to go out shooting craps next Thursday – and I've no idea how to cook them.'

✪

251. My husband's cooking is so bad that when he cooks for a dinner party the guests pray before the meal – and after it.

✪

252. My wife's cakes are so stodgy and heavy that when I throw them out for the birds to eat, the birds then have to *walk* South for the winter.

✪

253. When his wife read the recipe instructions to separate two eggs, she kept one in the kitchen and put one in the lounge.

✪

254. The overworked woman called to her husband and children: 'Your dinner is on the table – I've been too busy to put it on plates.'

✪

CORONER

255. In order to become a coroner you have to take a stiff exam.

✪

COUNSELLING

256. The priest was beginning to feel that he had chosen the wrong profession, so he went to a counsellor for advice.

'Just for once,' suggested the counsellor, 'remove all your trappings of the priesthood and go up to the city tonight. Don't tell anyone you're a priest. Just look around you and see if you can have a good time. Then come back to me and we can discuss matters further.'

Thus it was that the priest found himself in a raunchy nightclub. He watched in amazement at the topless dancers. Then a voluptuous woman did an incredible striptease right in front of where he was sitting. When she was down to her G-string she bent over him, her breasts just a few inches from his face, and she whispered: 'Hello, Father Thomas.'

'How do you know who I am?' asked the stunned priest.

The nearly-naked woman said: 'I'm Sister Clare. We probably have the same counsellor.'

❂

257. James went to a counsellor and said: 'I hope you can help me. My wife is very unfaithful. Every evening she goes out to the same bar and picks up men. She'll have sex with anyone who asks her – no matter what they look like. What can I do?'

The counsellor looked at James and said: 'Don't worry. Now, what was the name of that bar?'

❂

CREDITORS
258. The difference between creditors and debtors is that debtors *know* they owe money, whereas most creditors *think* they are going to get the money they are owed.

❂

CRIME AND CRIMINALS
259. Last night a man broke a fishmonger's window and stole all the crustaceans. It was a smash and *crab* raid.

❂

260. 'Hey!' shouted a policeman to a man just emerging late one night from a dress shop. 'Stop right there!'

The policeman went up to the man who slumped to the ground outside the shop. The man was clutching a box containing a blue dress.

'I have reason to suspect that you have just stolen that dress,' said the policeman. 'And I must say that shop seems very popular with you burglars. This is the third night in a row that it's been robbed.'

'I know,' said the burglar. 'My wife is very fussy about her appearance and keeps changing her mind about what she wants to wear – she made me come back again tonight because she went off the dresses I got earlier.'

✪

261. Her mother was a shoplifter. Unfortunately, she took after her.

✪

262. When she returned home from a party, Candy discovered that her house had been burgled. She quickly phoned the police and sat calmly until a police van arrived. As she went to open the front door, she saw a policeman with an Alsatian dog get out of the van. Candy burst into tears and sobbed: 'I've been burgled – and what do the police send? A blind cop with his guide dog.'

✪

263. John had been in prison for only three months when he got into a fight with another prisoner who sliced off John's ear with a knife. A short time later he got tonsillitis and had his tonsils removed. Then John got a mouth infection and had to have six teeth extracted. Soon after that, his hand got slammed in a door and he had to have the tips of three fingers amputated.

A few weeks later John had appendicitis and his appendix was taken out. It was at this point that a prison warder went to the governor of the prison and warned: 'I think John is escaping bit by bit.'

✪

264. When he arrived home looking tired and exhausted, the judge sighed and told his wife: 'It's been another trying day.'

✪

265. The prosecution lawyer was questioning the defendant. 'You took money from friends, relatives and work colleagues telling them that you would invest it on their behalf. Yet instead of investing it, you used it to live the high life. How could you take money from people who trusted you?'

The defendant looked at the lawyer and said: 'Isn't it obvious? Who else would give me money? People who didn't trust me would be unlikely to give me any.'

❀

266. What happened to the woman who was caught stealing a battery?

She was put in a dry cell.

❀

267. He thought the judge was being lenient in giving him a suspended sentence – until he was taken out of the courtroom and led to the gallows.

❀

268. Yesterday I was standing in a queue in a fast food restaurant when a man pointed a gun at a counter assistant and said: 'Give me all the money in your till.'

The counter assistant asked: 'Will that be to use here, or to take away?'

❀

269. Late last night a large quantity of sand and cement were stolen from a builder's yard. Police are hunting for some concrete evidence.

❀

270. When the burglars broke into his house they could see that his wife had left him. The house plants were all dead and the only sign of life was the stuff growing in the refrigerator.

❀

271. Philip was sent to prison for making big money. He made it half a centimetre too big.

❀

272. When the policeman caught Fred stealing a lady's undergarment from a washing line, Fred pleaded with the cop not to arrest him, saying: 'It was my first slip.'

❀

273. When she was asked why she had killed her husband by using a bow and arrow, she explained: 'I didn't want to make a noise and wake the kids.'

❀

274. He used to be a burglar – but it was his short-sightedness that got him caught. Late one night he climbed into a house through an open window. He could hear sounds of gentle snoring from people asleep in the bed-rooms so he made his way silently to the lounge. He twiddled some knobs on what he thought was the safe – and the radio blared out loud music.

❀

275. Mr and Mrs Jones were just coming out of the hotel car park when they saw their car being driven away.

'Stop thief!' shouted Mr Jones. As the car sped away, he turned to his wife and asked: 'Did you get a good look at the driver? Could you describe him to the police?'

'No,' replied Mrs Jones. 'But I did manage to remember the licence number of the car.'

❀

276. The burglar was careful to wear close-fitting pigskin gloves when he broke into an office and cracked open the safe. The next day the police were on the scene, made a lot of tests and a short time later arrested a hog in Wisconsin.

❀

277. The local flasher was getting on in years and so decided to retire. Then he changed his mind and thought he would stick it out for another year.

❀

278. Three convicted criminals are being taken from a courthouse to prison when the prison van is involved in an accident. Seizing their chance, the three criminals break out of the van and run off down the street.

Police dogs are soon called in and one of the criminals suggests that in order to put the dogs off their scent they should hide in the zoo. The smell from all the animals would surely confuse the dogs.

Climbing over the wall into the zoo, the three criminals soon see a large warehouse-like building. Inside, they see sacks of food for the animals and a number of boxes with small air holes. The boxes contain various creatures that have recently been transported to the zoo. Two of the criminals each find themselves an empty box and conceal themselves inside.

Some time later, several policemen enter the building and look around. One of the policemen looks at a box on which has been printed: 'Wild Cat.' He taps the box. The criminal inside the box goes: 'Meow, meow.'

The police check a number of the other boxes by tapping on them. Then they tap on the side of a box in which another criminal is hiding. On the side of that box is printed: 'Wild pig.' The criminal inside goes: 'Oink. Oink.'

Then the police decide to check on the sacks containing food for the animals. As one policeman kicks a sack labelled 'Vegetables', the criminal inside says: 'Vegetables. Vegetables.'

D

DATING

279. He's just found the perfect girl to take to the dance – he's got two left feet and she's got two right feet.

❀

280. When the elderly gentleman was asked how he managed to go out with so many young, beautiful women, he said that it was because of the wonderful smell of his aftershave – it smelt like money.

❀

281. I can't understand what women see in Percy. He's not very attractive, he's quite short and he wears spectacles. When he goes to a club he just has to sit with a glass of wine and women flock to him – despite his strange habit of licking his left ear with his tongue.

❀

282. I recently joined a dating agency and said I wanted to meet someone small and cute and who liked climbing and the outdoor life. It would also be good if her favourite foods were similar to mine: nuts and fruit. They matched me up with a squirrel.

❀

283. When someone told me they had seen a beautiful woman on Jeremy's arm I said: 'He's never showed me that tattoo.'

❀

284. The reason it is so difficult for women to find men who are good looking, sensitive and caring is because such men already have boyfriends.

❀

285. Jeremy had managed to get a girl to have dinner with him. After an expensive meal in a romantic restaurant, with the girl having had rather too much to drink, Jeremy walked with her to her front door.

Throughout the evening he had not dared touch her. Standing by her door he looked at her nervously.

'Do you shrink from kissing?' asked the girl.

'No,' replied Jeremy: 'I've always been short.'

❁

286. Last night he met a woman in a bar. He chatted to her and soon they were kissing and cuddling. Then they went outside and walked towards her car where their passion increased. She took out her car key, kissed him passionately and told him: 'You can have anything you want.' So he took the key and her car.

❁

287. One of my friends has a great zest for life but she is very old. She doesn't date men her own age because there are no men that age.

❁

288. When he got a woman to come to his apartment he managed to bring out the animal in her. Soon after arriving she was running to the door and scratching and whining to get out.

❁

289. When men are looking around a bar for a woman to try to seduce, the ones they are most interested in are those that are breathing.

❁

290. When he at last managed to get a girl, as he caressed her cheek, she caressed his cheque.

❁

291. Laura was having a quick lunch in a café when a handsome young man asked if he could join her as the other tables were fully occupied.

'Sure,' replied Laura.

The young man introduced himself as Jamie and they were soon deep in conversation.

After an enjoyable lunch Jamie asked: 'Can I see you again tonight?'

'I'm sorry,' replied Laura, 'but I've already agreed to go to an all-girl party tonight.'

'How about a date on Saturday?' asked Jamie.

'I'm sorry again,' said Laura. 'I'm getting married on Saturday. But we could make a date for the following Saturday.'

❀

292. He was so desperate for romance that he read all the lonely hearts advertisements in the newspapers and sent off letters and copies of his photo to many of them. They all returned his photo with a note saying they were not *that* lonely.

❀

293. She said that the trouble with blind dates is that they are rather like snowstorms – you never know how many inches you'll get or how long they will last.

❀

294. It was their first date. They appeared to have had a nice time – a pleasant meal, a visit to the theatre, and a nice stroll to her home.

As they stood outside her door he moved closer to her, gazed at her face and asked: 'Will I see you pretty soon?'

She pushed him away and asked, in an angry/hurtful tone: 'What? Don't you think I'm pretty *now*?'

❀

295. After going out on lots of dates Joe believes that the difference between a slut and a bitch is that a slut will sleep with anyone and everyone. But a bitch will sleep with anyone but him.

❀

296. When Jeremy eventually managed to get a girl to go out with him he took her to an expensive restaurant and, to impress her, ordered the whole meal in French. The girl and the waiter were amazed by this – especially as the restaurant was Chinese.

❀

297. I recently went out with a feminist and when I heard a plane overhead I looked up and said: 'That's the mail plane.' She stamped her feet and said: 'It's so high up how can you possibly tell what sex it is?'

❀

298. 'Mum, I'm fed up,' said Cora. 'Why do we have to live in such a small village? And why does Dad have such a lecherous reputation? So far I've fancied nine handsome young men. Yet every time I bring one of them home for dinner, Dad later takes me aside and warns me not to take things too far because the man is really my half-brother. Aren't there *any* eligible men in the village?'

'Don't worry,' said Cora's mother. 'Any of the last three young men you brought home would have been suitable. He doesn't know it, but your father is not your *real* father.'

✿

DENTIST

299. A very posh lady lived in a large house in a small village. When several of her teeth began to ache she went to the dentist who explained the treatment she needed and said he was going to give her a local anaesthetic.

In plummy tones, the posh lady said: 'What? A *local* anaesthetic. But I'm a private patient. Give me one from London.'

✿

300. The patient was complaining to his dentist about the cost of removing a bad tooth: 'You charge a lot of money for what will probably only take you a few minutes.'

'Well,' said the dentist, 'if you like I can pull the tooth very, very slowly and take an hour.'

✿

301. The man was ushered into a chair by the dental assistant who told the dentist: 'This is Mr Bacon.'

The dentist looked at Mr Bacon and said: 'Lean back, please.'

✿

DESERT ISLAND

302. He was alone on a desert island with only coconuts and figs to eat. At first, he ate only the coconuts and became extremely constipated. As the weeks went by his stomach grew to huge proportions as his bowels failed to move. He felt very uncomfortable so, in desperation, he ate lots of figs. They caused a violent reaction inside his body where gases built up and he exploded. Thus, on the desert island he had been shit-wrecked.

❀

DIETS
303. Her doctor told her she should stop having intimate dinners for four – unless there were three other people with her.

❀

304. She said she couldn't possibly go on a celebrity diet. She didn't want to eat famous people.

❀

305. I know a woman who went on what is called the 'Hollywood Actress Diet' – three males a day.

❀

306. The secret of successful dieting is said to be the triumph of mind over platter.

❀

DIVORCE
307. The greatest cause of divorce is marriage.

❀

308. John got tired of his wife forever picking on him and being argumentative. He was therefore glad to divorce her. Unfortunately, when he slipped behind with his maintenance payments she repossessed him.

❀

DOCTOR
309. Mrs Jones handed over her full urine sample container to the doctor. He started to write on the label – but then stopped and sniffed. Opening the container he said: 'This isn't urine – it's apple juice.'

'Oh my goodness!' cried Mrs Jones. 'Can I use your phone? I urgently need to contact my son's school about the lunchbox I gave him this morning.'

❀

310. When Richard reached 50 he found that he always felt tired in the morning and afternoon, so he went to the doctor for advice.

After a physical examination and answering all the doctor's questions, the doctor said: 'You've been over-exerting yourself sexually. You say you have sex at least twice every night. I suggest you give up sex one night a week – say, on Wednesdays.'

'Oh,' said Richard, 'I couldn't give up sex on Wednesdays – that's the night I do it with my wife.'

❀

311. When he asked a doctor: 'Can you give me something for my head?' the doctor looked at him and said: '*Give* you something for it? I wouldn't even take it if you gave it to me for free.'

❀

312. A woman phoned her doctor and said: 'Doctor, you've got to help me. My husband thinks he's a refrigerator.'

The doctor told her not to worry. He was rather busy dealing with a flu epidemic and suggested that as her husband didn't appear to be harming anyone, he would come out and see him in a few days' time.

'But doctor,' said the woman. 'Can't you do anything *now*? He keeps opening and closing his mouth in his sleep – and the little light coming on and going off keeps waking me up.'

❀

313. Last year I got ill. Since then I've been making payments on a Mercedes, a yacht and a villa in Spain – my doctors bought them.

❀

314. I've just met a man who said he was a privates investigator. 'Don't you mean a *private* investigator?' I asked.

'No,' he replied, 'I'm a gynaecologist.'

❀

315. Sally went to the doctor for an examination. 'You're pregnant,' said the doctor.

'Oh!' said Sally. 'Are you sure the baby is mine?'

❀

316. When he went to the doctor and said he thought he was suffering from amnesia, the doctor asked him to pay in advance.

❀

317. 'Doctor,' said the not very bright young man, 'my body hurts wherever I touch it.'

'Let me see,' said the doctor. 'Take off your shirt and show me where it hurts.'

The young man took off his shirt and touched his chest. 'It hurts here,' he said. Then he touched his stomach and said 'and it hurts here. No matter where I touch, it hurts. Even my legs.'

'Let me see your hand,' said the doctor. 'Ah!' said the doctor, examining the man's hand. 'You've got a broken index finger.'

❀

318. Mavis had tried many times to get pregnant, but without success, so she went to her doctor and asked him for advice.

'Just get undressed and lie down,' said the doctor, pointing to the bed in his surgery.

'Oh!' said Mavis. 'It's kind of you to offer, but I'd much prefer to have my husband's baby.'

❀

319. When the doctors went on strike and picketed the Department of Health they didn't have much effect: no one could read their writing on the picket signs.

❀

320. Paul went to the doctor to complain about a ringing noise in his ears. 'It's rather like a telephone,' he said. 'What can I do?'

The doctor examined Paul's ears and said: 'Have you tried getting your head an unlisted number?'

❀

321. He's so stupid, when the doctor asked him to get a stool sample he went home and sawed a bit off one of the legs on the kitchen stool.

❀

322. Like his father, Peter was a doctor. One day, when his father was away from the surgery, Peter attended to Charles, a patient who visited the practice regularly.

Peter had told his father that he had examined Charles and looked at his father's medical notes. It seemed the man's ailments had been caused by the pills prescribed by his father. Peter had not informed Charles of this, but had simply told him that the pills appeared to have strength-ened Charles's immunity over the years and, once he had finished his existing supply, there was no need to take the pills again.

'You fool!' snapped Peter's father. 'I didn't make a mistake prescribing those pills. It was because he had those pills he kept coming to the surgery as a private patient. It was his fees that helped to put you through medical school.'

❁

323. Harry looked very fit and healthy. He was also incredibly wealthy and had summoned a doctor to visit him.

As the doctor made his way to Harry's mansion he wondered what the problem could be. Harry seemed to live the ideal life. Everything he wanted he could get at the touch of a button: from controlling his vast TV/entertainment system to ordering food. Just by press-ing buttons he could summon one of his maids, or the valet or his masseur. He could even lie in bed and press a button that made the roof slide open so he could gaze at the stars.

On arrival at the mansion he found Harry looking forlorn and wailing: 'My finger hurts!'

❁

324. An apple a day keeps the doctor away – bad breath and body odour will keep the rest of the people away.

❁

325. The young doctor had just been on a course on how to handle patients in a friendly and non-demeaning man-ner. Even if someone came to see him smelling like a sewer he was expected not to show his emotions or refer to a foul stench but should try to let the patient make the first reference to the smell. At all times, he should try to put patients at ease.

A few days after the course, a huge lady knocked on the door to his surgery. He was delighted when she began the conversation by saying: 'Doctor, I think I'm a bit over-weight.'

'That's OK,' soothed the doctor, remembering his training, 'just pull up three chairs and let's talk about it.'

❀

DOGS
326. My dog keeps making mistakes – he's a cock-up spaniel.

❀

327. What's got four legs and an arm?
An angry dog.

❀

328. Last year he bought a watch dog. It proved to be an excellent watch dog as it watched someone break into the garden shed and steal all the garden tools, then it watched someone steal the car from the driveway, and then it watched the house burn down.

❀

329. I know a man who called his dog Rolex because it was a watch dog.

❀

330. When I visited my young nephew I noticed that his dog was scratching. 'Does your dog have fleas?' I asked.
My nephew looked at me scornfully and replied: 'Surely you know that dogs don't have fleas – they have puppies.'

❀

331. It took me six months, but at last I've taught my dog to beg. Last night he came home with enough money to buy us both a decent meal.

❀

332. George loved his dog Pluck. He had given it that name after he had found it, abandoned as a puppy, by the side of a busy road. The puppy had been malnourished and suffered various skin and other infections, but had bravely fought to survive. George had nursed it back to health.

The dog was a faithful companion and loved playing games with George. His favourite game was to bark wildly as George threw a rubber bone for the dog to chase and then bring back to George. For years they had played this game happily, although a new neighbour had complained about the noise of the barking.

Now Pluck was old and his eyesight was failing. How could the dog continue to play such games if it could not see where the bone had landed?

Then George had an idea. He remembered the cards he had received at Christmas and birthdays which, when they were opened, played a tune. He would create a similar sort of device, but using a voice synthesiser, for incorporation in a bone. When the bone hit the ground it would trigger the mechanism to keep repeating the dog's name. George knew that Pluck's hearing was still very good, so the dog would only need to follow the sound from the bone to find it. Then George could call for the dog to return to him and hope the dog would also bring back the bone.

George spent several weeks making various experimental bones until he felt he had achieved his goal. Now was the time for a real test. He took the bone into the garden and threw it. Unfortunately, George, too, was getting old and his aim was not as good as it once was, and the bone soared over the garden fence and landed in his neighbour's garden. Even worse, the sound device inside the bone malfunctioned and instead of repeating 'Pluck' kept repeating an offensive four-letter word that begins with 'F' and rhymes with Pluck.

The neighbour was outraged and phoned the police. Poor George was then arrested and charged with making obscene bone calls.

❀

DOPE

333. She wanted to grow her own dope – so she planted a man.

❀

DREAMS

334. I dream in colour – but it may be a pigment of my imagination.

❀

335. The man from London said: 'I don't need anyone to interpret my dreams – I dream in English.'

❀

E

EAST EUROPEAN

336. When the elderly East European lady was asked if she had heard of Red Riding Hood she replied: 'Isn't that a Russian condom?'

✿

ECONOMISTS

337. A government economist is someone who not only doesn't know what he is talking about – but he makes you feel it is all your fault.

✿

338. The reason economic forecasters exist is to make weather forecasters look good by comparison.

✿

339. The only thing economic forecasters don't assume is responsibility.

✿

EROTIC

340. He thinks it's erotic to suck women's toes. That's why he quite often asks women to step into his orifice.

✿

341. The difference between erotic and kinky is that in the first you make use of a feather – but with kinky you use the whole duck.

✿

EVENING CLASSES

342. David was telling his friend John about how much he enjoyed going to evening classes.

'What are you studying?' asked John.

'Current affairs,' said David. 'It's really great. You should come along, too.'

'No,' said John. 'I don't need to study that – I get all the knowledge I need from the TV news.'

'OK.' said David. 'Can you tell me the name of the President of France? Or who is the Prime Minister of Canada? Or name the Russian President?'

John admitted that he could not answer the questions, then asked: 'But do *you* know who Algernon Arbuthnot Snotsworth-Sizzletone is?'

'No,' replied David. 'Who is he?'

'He's the man,' said John, 'who visits your wife when you are out at your evening classes.'

☺

EXCITEMENT

343. She was so excited. At the weekend a handsome young man took her up the aisle . . . and showed her to her seat in the cinema.

☺

EXERCISE

344. My husband is getting rather plump, so this summer I'm taking him to the beach for some exercise to reduce the size of his belly. I know I'll never get him to swim, jog or play games – so I'm taking him to the part of the beach that has the most beautiful girls in bikinis.

Then, every time one of the girls walks near him, he'll breathe in and hold his stomach in until she walks past. Then he'll breathe out again until the next girl moves near. I reckon he'll do these deep breathing stomach exercises at least a hundred times a day.

☺

345. My wife recently joined an aerobics class and she gets a lot of exercise. She's never actually managed to get to the class – but she spends a tremendous amount of time and energy trying to put on her leotard.

☺

346. If God had wanted me to touch my toes he would have put them on my thighs.

☺

347. The only exercise he gets is jumping to wrong conclusions.

☺

348. Why do people keep going on and on about getting more exercise? Why spend an hour a day working out in the gym or jogging? You could spend the time doing something else that's much more enjoyable while you're still young enough to do it. All that extra exercise will do is possibly give you an extra year or two when you're old and cost you a fortune in extra nursing home fees.

☻

349. My wife keeps telling me to get in shape. But I told her I *am* in shape – *round* is a shape.

☻

F

FAIRYLAND

350. He tried to become President of Fairyland. His speeches were wildly applauded by the pixies and fairies, but he failed to impress the elves. This made him very depressed and he began to suffer from low *elf*-esteem.

✿

FALSE TEETH

351. George was delighted the day he got his first set of false teeth. Even his young children said the teeth made him look years younger.

That evening George had a lot of work to do in his study, so by the time he went to bed he was feeling very tired. As he bent towards the bedside table to set his alarm clock, George realised he was still wearing his false teeth. He felt too weary to get out of bed and go to the bathroom to put the teeth in a glass of water, so he just removed the teeth and put them on the bedside table.

The following morning the teeth had disappeared. George looked behind the bedside table, under the bed, queried the children as to the whereabouts of his missing teeth – but the teeth could not be found.

Later that day he was making his bed and, lifting up the pillow, saw a pile of coins resting on the sheet. The tooth fairy had taken his false teeth by mistake.

✿

FARMERS

352. I was driving through the countryside the other day and suddenly I noticed several chickens running along the side of the road. I looked at my speedometer. It was incredible. I was travelling at fifty miles per hour – and yet the chickens were managing to keep up with the car. Then I noticed that each chicken had six legs.

Soon I came to a farm which displayed a notice: 'Eggs for sale.' I drove into the farmyard and spoke to the farmer: 'I've just seen some amazing chickens. They appear to have six legs.'

'Yes,' replied the farmer. 'They're genetically modified chickens. The idea is that from one bird you get six chicken-leg dinners.'

'Amazing,' I said. 'What do they taste like?'

'I've no idea,' replied the farmer. 'We've never been fast enough to catch one.'

☺

353. An old man and his young grandson were walking along the road with their donkey. All of them were quite happy, although the donkey was carrying a load of lettuces from their farm.

A car approached them and stopped. The driver, a middle-aged woman from the town, opened the car window and shouted: 'You're cruel! Making that poor donkey carry such a heavy load is wicked!'

'But we're only going to the market to sell the lettuces,' said the old man.

'The market is too far away for such a poor animal,' said the woman. 'If you make the donkey walk all that way carrying all those lettuces you should be prosecuted for cruelty to animals.'

As the woman drove away, the old man sighed. The donkey, the old man and the grandson continued towards the town, but when they reached the next farm they saw that the farmer was loading a large lorry with a crop of lettuces.

'Would you like to buy my lettuces?' asked the old man. A deal was hastily done.

The price the farmer paid for the lettuces was much less than the old man would have made if he had sold them in the market. But at least the old man could no longer be accused of cruelty to the donkey.

As they journeyed back towards their home, the grandson sat on the donkey. Walking towards them was a priest who stopped and said to the small boy: 'Have you no respect for your elders? Why are you riding on the donkey when you have a young pair of legs while this poor old man has to struggle to walk. You should change places.'

The old man and the grandson agreed to swap places and they continued on their journey home. Soon a car approached, slowed down and stopped. The male driver shouted out to the old man: 'Outrageous! Why are you, a grown man, riding on the donkey and making this poor little boy walk?'

'But I don't mind walking,' said the grandson.

'Nonsense!' snapped the man in the car. 'That man probably beats you so you will say things like that. I shall report him for cruelty to children.'

The car driver carried out his threat and the old man was hauled into court. He pleaded not guilty, but the court system and the lawyers kept delaying the hearing then, when the case eventually came to court, it was postponed for reports from social workers. When the matter came to court again the lawyers got an adjournment so certain legal issues could be investigated. Eventually, almost a year later, the case came to trial and the old man was acquitted.

Unfortunately, in order to pay all his legal costs, the old man had to sell his farm – including all the animals. When a neighbouring farmer came to take away his donkey, the old man was in tears as he loved that animal.

The moral of this sad tale is that if you try to please all of the people all of the time you will have to kiss your ass goodbye!

❂

354. A farmer friend of mine keeps telling jokes to chickens. He's hoping to turn them into comedi-hens. At least they might appreciate corny jokes . . .

❂

355. My young cousin lives on a farm and was given a pet duck for his birthday. He was soon proudly boasting that the duck could say its own name.

'What *is* the duck's name?' I asked.

My cousin replied: 'Its name is Quack.'

✪

356. Jake and his son Gabriel were farmers. From birth, they had lived in a small, remote village surrounded by mountains. Due to its location, television reception was impossible.

Jake and Gabriel had never even visited a town – let alone a major city. But all that was to change when they received a letter from a lawyer stating that they were the major beneficiaries under a distant relative's will. They were asked to attend a meeting with the lawyer in the city.

Jake and Gabriel were rather nervous about visiting a large, crowded city, but eventually they arrived at the multi-storey office block housing the lawyer's firm.

As they waited in reception, Jake saw an elderly, very wrinkled woman press a button on one of the walls. Two metal doors slid open and the woman got in, pressed the number 21, and the doors closed.

A display panel above the doors showed numbers that started to count up to 21, then paused for a while before dropping rapidly. When the numbers stopped to be replaced by the letter G, the metal doors opened and a beautiful young woman walked out into the reception area.

'Did you see that?' Gabriel asked his son. 'We must bring your mother here. I wonder how much it would cost to put her in that contraption and make her look 21 so quickly.'

✪

FATHER FIGURE

357. A lot of young woman treat him as a father figure – they ask him for money.

✪

FIRING SQUAD

358. He was just about to be shot by a firing squad when the rebel leader asked him: 'Do you have any last requests?'

'Yes,' replied the captive. 'Can I sing a song?'

The rebel leader thought for a few seconds, then said: 'OK. Start singing.'

The captive started: 'There were ten million green bottles standing on a wall . . .'

✿

359. Bernard was standing with his back to a wall. Facing him was a firing squad.

'Would you like a cigarette?' asked the leader of the firing squad.

'No thanks,' replied Bernard. 'I'm giving them up for health reasons.'

✿

360. Two men were captured by rebels and were to be killed by firing squad. The rebel leader kicked one of the captured men and said: 'You are first to be shot. Do you have any last requests?'

'Yes, said the man. 'I love rap music. Can you play one of the rap CDs you took from my bag over your loud-speaker system?'

The rebel leader replied: 'We can do that. In fact, I quite like rap music myself. Maybe we can play two or three tracks.'

The second captured man then said: 'Please! If you are going to do that then my last request is to be shot first.'

✿

FROGS

361. A frog went to a fortune teller who told him: 'Soon you will meet a beautiful young girl. She will be interested in finding out all about you – and will show you to her friends and . . .'

The frog was so happy and excited, he interrupted the fortune teller to ask: 'Will I meet her at the pond?'

'No,' replied the fortune teller. 'She will meet you when you are taken to her biology lesson.'

✿

362. Two very elderly women, Gladys and Mabel, were walking slowly in the park when Gladys suddenly heard a croaking voice call: 'Stop! Help!' Looking down she saw she had nearly stepped on a frog.

'Oh!' said Gladys to her companion. 'Look at that – a frog!'

As the two women stared at the frog, the frog said: 'Can one of you please help me? I'm a handsome young man and I have been turned into a frog by a wicked witch. If you kiss me I'll turn back into a handsome young man and I'll make love to you any way you want.'

'Well, dear,' said Mabel to Gladys, 'you saw the frog first so it's only right you can have it.'

'Thank you,' said Gladys, picking up the frog and putting it in her handbag.

Mabel was surprised. 'Aren't you going to kiss it?' she asked.

'No, I don't think so,' replied Gladys. 'At my age I think I'd get more fun from keeping a talking frog.'

❂

363. When frogs tell bedtime stories to their children, how do the stories end?

With the words 'and then the ugly prince turned into a beautiful frog'.

❂

FUNERAL
364. When he asked to buried at sea, his family hired a team of divers to dig his grave.

❂

365. When the woman renowned for her sexual exploits with numerous men finally died of a heart attack, hundreds of people attended her funeral.

As the coffin was lowered into the grave one of the mourners said: 'Together at last.'

'With her husband?' asked the lady standing next to him.

'No,' replied the mourner. 'At last both her legs are together.'

❂

366. The word 'funeral' begins with 'fun' – so why aren't funerals fun?

❂

367. The writer of television soap operas had grown very old, so he went to see the vicar of his local church to discuss funeral arrangements and to declare his firm belief in reincarnation. After much persuasion, and a large donation to church funds, the vicar agreed that the writer's tombstone could be inscribed: 'To be continued . . .'

❂

G

GENE POOL

368. The main problem with the gene pool is that there don't seem to be any lifeguards.

❁

369. He said that he and his ancestors had not fought for many thousands of years to get to the top of the gene pool in order to be vegetarians.

❁

GENERALIST

370. A 'generalist' is someone who generally knows nothing about everything.

❁

GENIE

371. The noise and smell were unbearable. Everywhere he looked all Joshua could see were male deer. They were in every room of his house, soiling the carpet, messing up the beds, destroying the kitchen. The creatures were packed into his garage and his garden. The whole street where he lived in a small town in the USA was crowded with the male deer.

Joshua cursed the genie he had released from a bottle earlier that day. Joshua had discovered the bottle when he had been clearing out the cellar. The genie had offered Joshua one wish – which the genie had clearly misunderstood. 'Why,' sighed Joshua, 'didn't I specify a million US *dollars* instead of asking for a million *bucks*?'

❁

372. Last week I was walking along the beach when I saw an old bottle sticking out of the sand. Fearing it might cause someone to trip I pulled it from the sand and as I did so the top came off the bottle and an elderly genie popped out.

'How can I help you?' asked the genie. 'I have been stuck in this bottle for many, many years as the waves carried me many miles.'

'Do I get three wishes?' I asked.

'Sorry,' replied the genie. 'But I am so old most of my powers have gone. I no longer have the power to give you eternal life or a fortune in gold. But I could probably manage a more modest request.'

'How about a date with an attractive film star?' I asked.

'Certainly!' replied the genie. 'It is done' – and he vanished in a puff of smoke.

Two days later a large limousine drew up outside my house, a uniformed chauffeur got out and said he was taking me to town for a surprise meeting with a film star. I was really excited throughout the journey. On arrival at an expensive hotel I was escorted to a suite where, lying on a sofa, was my date – Lassie.

❀

GHOSTS

373. I know a beautiful female ghost who used to have her photo on the front pages of glossy magazines. She was a cover ghoul.

❀

374. I was woken in the night by strange crashing sounds coming from the kitchen. I crept downstairs and saw a strange apparition throwing crockery on the floor. It looked like the ghost of a giant chicken – it was a poultry-geist.

❀

GIRLFRIENDS

375. His new girlfriend looks just like a model. She's not young, tall, leggy and beautiful – but has *real* model looks: She's very small and appears to be made of plastic.

❀

376. When her boyfriend asked her how she got such shapely eyebrows she said: 'It takes a lot of pluck.'

❀

377. Last night my son brought home a girl whom he introduced as his new girlfriend. She was extremely ugly and so I quietly took my son to one side and asked: 'Is she *really* your girlfriend?'

'Yes,' he replied. 'She's all I can get when I don't have a car of my own and you won't let me drive yours.'

❀

378. My girlfriend and I have just broken up. It was all due to astrological circumstances. She was a water sign and I'm an earth sign, so our relationship soon turned to mud.

❀

379. My girlfriend has been out with lots of other men so some people say she was a sleep-around tramp. I prefer to think of her as a previously-used woman.

❀

380. Last night my girlfriend snuggled up to me, rubbed her hands over my body and said: 'Whisper my favourite word in my ear,' so I did as she requested and said: 'Money!'

❀

381. He said he almost had a psychic girlfriend – but she left before they could meet.

❀

382. When I came home from work my girlfriend threw her arms around me and said: 'Darling, I'm so glad you're home. Now let's go out and do things.'

I kissed her passionately, then said: 'Why don't we stay home and *undo* things?'

❀

383. One of my friends has just broken off his relationship with a young woman. I was rather surprised as he had been going out with her for six months and they seemed very happy together. But my friend explained the reason for the break-up. He said she had suddenly started using 'dreadful four-letter words' – like 'ring', 'baby' . . .

❀

384. Last night as my girlfriend and I were making love, her mobile phone rang. She picked it up and answered it, saying: 'Hello? Can I call you back later? I've got my boyfriend on hold.'

✿

385. I had to split-up with my girlfriend. She was beautiful, worked as a teacher, and we had a lot in common, but one of her habits was just too annoying. Whenever I sent her a love letter she would send it back with all the spelling and grammar corrected.

✿

386. His girlfriend has nice even teeth. 1, 3, 5, 7, 9, 11 and 13 are missing.

✿

387. Joe, Bruce and Charles were talking about their girlfriends.

'My Chrissie is wonderful,' said Bruce. 'Last night we made love three times. This morning, before she left for work, she left a note on the pillow saying how much she loves me and can't wait to get home to me tonight.'

'My Clare is unbelievable,' said Charles. 'She'll do anything in bed – and last night we made love four times – and this morning she said she'll think of me all day.'

'I love my Sally,' said Joe. 'Last night we made love and . . .'

'How many times?' asked Bruce and Charles.

'Once,' replied Joe.

'Only once?' asked Bruce.

'Did she say anything in the morning?' asked Charles.

'Yes,' replied Joe. "She said: 'I know we've been doing it all night long and it's so fantastic I wish we didn't have to stop to go to work.'"

✿

388. Keith was beginning to feel rather insecure. He felt sure that there was something his girlfriend was not telling him. Keith loved her deeply – but was she playing around with another man?

As his concerns grew, Keith decided he had to do something. When his girlfriend invited him to her apartment he waited until she was in the bathroom and then raced to her bedroom. Opening the top drawer of her dressing table, all he could find were cosmetics, jewellery and hair care products.

Opening another drawer he looked at her large selection of panties and other lingerie – but rummaging around in the drawer he felt something hard. Pulling it from the underwear he saw that it was a framed photo of a handsome young man.

At that point, Keith's girlfriend entered the room. 'What are you doing?' she asked.

'Just checking your underwear drawer,' replied Keith. 'I'd like to buy you something special and I was just making sure I'd get the correct size.'

'You're so kind,' said his girlfriend, putting her arms around him. 'Let's go to bed.'

After they had made love, Keith gently stroked his girlfriend's cheek. 'I don't really know how to ask this – but am I your only boyfriend?'

'Of course you are!' said his girlfriend, kissing him passionately.

'And you don't have any secret feelings for anyone else?' asked Keith.

'No,' said his girlfriend. 'You're the only man for me. But why are you suddenly asking me about other men?'

'Well,' said Keith, 'when I was looking in your underwear drawer I found a framed photo of a man. He looked quite handsome. Who is he?'

'Darling,' said the girlfriend. '*He* doesn't exist any more. The photo is of me before I had the operation.'

❀

GOLF
389. What's the difference between a bad golfer and a bad skydiver?

A bad golfer goes: *Whack!* 'Oh damn!' while a bad skydiver goes: 'Oh damn!' *Whack!*

❀

390. In order to advance his career, Sebastian decided to take up golf. After his first morning on the golf course his wife asked him: 'How did it go?'

'Seventy-two strokes!' said Sebastian.

'That's wonderful,' said his wife.

'It took me seventy-two strokes,' said Sebastian, 'just to hit the first ball.'

❀

391. It was a whirlwind romance. Within days, they were married. But he was a fanatical golf player, so on the day after their wedding he said to his wife: 'I hope you don't mind, but I have to go out. I promised to play in a golf tournament and I won't be back until late.'

'That's all right,' said his wife. 'I have to go out, too. And I'll be back late. I hope you don't mind, but I'm a hooker.'

'Oh,' said her husband. 'Is it your stance or your grip?'

❀

392. He went to his priest and asked: 'Is it a sin to play golf on Sunday?'

The priest replied: 'I've seen you on the golf course several times. The way you play it's a sin any day.'

❀

393. What is the difference between a golf ball and a woman's G-spot?

Men don't mind spending time finding the golf ball.

❀

394. 'I've had a lousy day,' said Brian to his wife when she returned from visiting her mother.

'But I thought you were going out on the golf course,' said his wife.

'I did,' replied Brian. 'And I hit my two very best balls – I trod on a rake.'

❀

395. I was walking past a golf course with my young cousin when he suddenly stopped and looked at a man who was struggling with a ball and beating at it in a bunker.

My cousin pointed and asked: 'What does he do after he's killed it?'

☸

396. The police arrested him for killing his wife with a golf club.

'Her injuries show that you hit her with the club nine times,' said one of the policeman.

'Oh,' said the arrested man, 'couldn't you put it down as a five or six?'

☸

397. Paul went to a golf club only to discover that his usual partner had been involved in a car accident and had been taken to hospital. However, a new club member offered to play with him.

After the first few holes, Paul was trailing behind. The new member said to Paul: 'You know, you could get a hole in one with your next shot. It may surprise you to know this, but I am a man with magical powers. You have to promise me something and I can grant wishes.'

'What sort of thing do I have to promise?' asked Paul.

'Well,' said the new member. 'Are you gay?'

'No,' replied Paul.

'Then,' said the new member, 'if you promise not to have sex with a woman for six months – you'll get a hole in one with your next shot. Promise you will never marry or have sexual relations with any woman or even touch a naked woman and I irrevocably guarantee that within a year you will be the best player in the whole club.'

'Done,' said Paul. 'I promise never to have such intimate contact with a woman.'

The new member muttered a strange incantation and, sure enough, Paul's next shot saw the ball fly straight into the hole, and Paul eventually won the game.

'Congratulations,' said the new member. 'Remember to keep your promise and what I guaranteed will surely happen. But, just for the record, can I make a note of your name and where you live?'

So Paul revealed that he was Father Paul O'Malley and lived in the house next to the Catholic church.

✿

H

HARD WORK

398. To all those people who keep telling me that 'hard work never hurt anyone' I would just like to ask: 'Name anyone who got hurt because they *didn't* do hard work.'

❂

HEAVEN AND HELL

399. Waiting outside the Pearly Gates to Heaven were a stockbroker and a priest.

The gates opened and St Peter went straight to the stockbroker, smiled broadly and said: 'Welcome! Welcome! Delighted to see you! Come right in.'

The stockbroker entered Heaven and was immediately surrounded by heavenly helpers who escorted him to a large room with a table laden with the finest food and wine. Harpists played while he enjoyed an excellent meal.

Meanwhile, St Peter had simply said to the priest: 'OK Come in. One of my assistants will show you to your dormitory.'

Some time later, when the priest was eating a frugal meal of bread, cheese, fruit and cheap wine, one of his fellow priests was telling him about the lavish treatment given to the stockbroker.

'St Peter even came to the broker and had a long conversation,' said the fellow priest. 'He thanked the broker for all that he had done.'

'That doesn't seem very fair,' said the newly arrived priest. 'I worked hard promoting God for over fifty years and devoted myself to helping my congregation. What did the stockbroker do to get such fantastic treatment? Give all his money to charity? Risk his life to save hundreds of people?'

'None of those things,' said the fellow priest. 'You preached religion, and persuaded perhaps a thousand people to pray to God, but most of them were religious anyway. You didn't actually convert that many people to the faith.

'The stockbroker preached about Mammon and persuaded *hundreds of thousands* of people to invest in highly speculative shares. As share prices plummeted, most of those investors were converted to the faith and prayed to God at least several times a day. They did it far more enthusiastically than the people you preached at. But don't worry, the broker was only here as a 'thank you' gesture for a day – then he was sent to somewhere much hotter.'

❂

400. Less than half a per cent of dead bagpipe players go to Heaven. That's because if any more went, it would be Hell.

❂

401. Clarissa and Clara were two elderly women who became friends while staying in an old folks' home in the country. They enjoyed each other's company.

Both ladies were widows and they would sometimes chat about how they missed sex, and even talked about their ideal men. But their conversations covered many topics – the latest political news, books they had read, the activities of their relatives.

Then one day Clarissa suddenly asked: 'Do you believe in Heaven and Hell?'

'I'm not too sure,' replied Clara. 'But if they do exist I wonder what they are really like. Is it like in some books with people riding around on clouds and playing harps? If so, the harp bit sounds a bit boring – I like more pacy music – guitars and sax and things.'

Clarissa thought for a moment and said: 'I believe very strongly that there is a Heaven. If I die first I'll try and send a message to you as to what it's actually like. Would you do the same for me if you should go first?'

Clara agreed. Three months later Clara died peacefully in her sleep.

The morning after Clara's funeral, Clarissa was woken by the sound of Clara's voice. Rubbing her eyes, Clarissa looked around her room, wondering if she would see a ghost. But there was no apparition, and Clara's voice said: 'Don't worry about dying. I'm having a wonderful time. I get lots of healthy food and the sex is simply incredible – I can get it as often and as many times a day as I like.'

'So you're in Heaven,' said Clarissa.

'No,' replied Clara. If you look outside your window you can see me. I've been reincarnated as a rabbit.'

❁

402. Mr and Mrs Smith's marriage had had its ups and downs. Although there had been fierce arguments when Mrs Smith's mother came to live with them, Mrs Smith was sad when her husband suddenly died.

A few months after his death Mrs Smith went to a séance at which a medium promised to put her in contact with Mr Smith.

After several minutes of rocking backwards and forwards and making strange noises, the medium began to talk in a voice like that of Mr Smith.

'How are you?' asked Mrs Smith.

'I'm fine,' replied her husband via the medium. 'It's great here. Even better than being at home with you and your mother.'

Mrs Smith sighed with relief and said: 'I'm *so* glad you went to Heaven.'

Her husband replied: 'Who said I was in Heaven?'

❁

HOLIDAYS

403. I was enjoying my holiday in the mountains when I heard loud cries of 'No! No! *No!*'

I looked around to see who was shouting and saw a man standing on the edge of a steep drop. I rushed to him as he continued to shout 'No! No! *No!*' and his words echoed back to him.

'Don't jump!' I shouted, fearing he was about to leap over the edge and kill himself.

He turned towards me and said: 'Don't worry, I'm not going to jump. I'm here for rest and relaxation.'

'Then why were you shouting "No! No! *No!*"' I asked.

'I like the echo,' he replied, 'and shouting gives me a great feeling of freedom. 'For eleven months of the year I *daren't* say "No". I'm a major corporation "yes-man".'

❀

404. When I was on holiday I suddenly saw a large tiger. At first, we just stared at each other – then it slowly moved towards me. I stood still and silent.

As the tiger got nearer it growled and then roared as it leapt straight towards me. But I stood my ground and did not flinch.

Then I moved away and went to look at the lions in the next cage in the zoo.

❀

405. Our safari holiday was very disappointing. The weather was terrible and the only game we saw were the locals playing snooker.

❀

406. A small boy was enjoying building a sandcastle with his father on the beach in Bournemouth.

'I'll get some water to fill the moat round the castle,' said the boy and took a plastic bucket and ran towards the sea. He found it great fun running in and out of the waves. Then he decided to collect some shells to decorate the castle.

After about fifteen minutes of wandering along the beach he suddenly realised he was lost. Fortunately, a lifeguard was nearby so the small boy went to him and said: 'Please can you help me? I've lost my Dad.'

The lifeguard looked at him reassuringly and asked: 'What's he like?'

'Beer and curries,' replied the boy.

❀

407. Last year on holiday we went to this strange place where there were lots of stalls with people hassling us to buy different types of jelly and custard – it was a trifle bazaar.

❁

408. Boris was on his first trip to a foreign country and was unsure of the travel procedures. When his plane arrived at his holiday destination he handed his landing card to an immigration officer.

The officer looked at the card and pointed to the space under 'sex' where Boris had written 'as often as possible.'

'That's not what we mean,' said the officer. 'We want you to put "male" or "female".'

Boris replied: 'It doesn't matter – either will do.'

❁

409. Brian had not enjoyed his first visit to a major foreign city. He had moaned about the traffic, the quality of the food, the people – so he was glad to be going home. However, at the airport he had to queue for hours to undergo an extensive security check. He moaned to one of the security people: 'This city is the asshole of the universe!'

'Well,' replied a security man, 'I understand you've just passed through.'

❁

410. He's such a worrier. When he went on holiday he sent his psychiatrist a postcard with the words: 'Having a wonderful time. Why?'

❁

411. I recently had a holiday in a country that was new to the tourist industry. I think that explains why, on my first night in my hotel, a maid knocked on my door and said: 'You tourists strange people.'

She then put her hand into a large pot that appeared to contain small pieces of meat. She took out some of it, held it over my bed and said: 'Manager tell me you like mince on your pillow.'

❁

412. Last summer I was trekking through a country in Africa when I came across a huge hippopotamus lying dead on the bank of a river. Somehow, the death did not look like natural causes. I turned to my guide and asked: 'Who killed the hippo?'

The guide shouted in a native language and a pygmy came out from behind a tree. 'Pygmy kill hippo,' said the guide.

'How can such a small person kill such a large creature?' I asked, and the guide translated my words to the pygmy and then translated his response: 'With a club.'

'It must have been a very large club,' I said.

'Yes,' replied the pygmy. 'There are over a hundred of us in it.'

❁

413. I was on a cruise liner and had to share a breakfast table with three couples: one from Jamaica, one from the US and one from a country that had better remain anonymous.

The Jamaican couple seemed deeply in love. They gazed into each other's eyes and there was much caressing. When the husband wanted some sugar, he asked his wife: 'Sugar, please pass the sugar.'

Seeing this, the American husband, also deeply in love, looked at his own wife and said: 'Honey, please pass the honey.'

This prompted the husband from the anonymous country to turn to his wife and say: 'Pass the bacon, pig.'

❁

414. When a friend asked her: 'Are you going on holiday with your husband and the kids?' she replied: 'No. I need a rest.'

❁

HONEYMOON

415. The 21-year-old woman walked stiffly to the breakfast room of the expensive hotel and slumped into a chair.

'Would you like some coffee?' asked a waiter. 'Or perhaps some soothing camomile tea?'

The young woman looked at him blankly. She looked completely exhausted.

'The tea, please,' she said. 'I just feel so incredibly tired. Every bone in my body aches and I was awake all night.'

The waiter smiled. 'Are you on honeymoon?' he asked.

'Yes,' replied the young woman. 'But my husband is 88 and when he told me he'd been saving up for seventy years – I thought he was referring to money.'

❀

416. Brian and his wife were having a second honeymoon and had booked into the London hotel where they had first made love during their courting days.

'Let's share a bath, like we did back then,' said Brian. His wife agreed and soon they were gently lowering themselves into the bath water.

'That's new,' said Brian, 'It's a spa bath.'

'No dear,' responded his wife, 'The bubbles are because you ate too much chilli and beans for dinner.'

❀

417. It was the first night of their honeymoon and the bride had accused her husband of getting drunk at the reception, being unnecessarily rude to her mother and passionately kissing one of the bridesmaids.

As she continued her complaining, the husband stormed out of their hotel room. Shortly afterwards, his wife regretted nagging and complaining so much. Her husband was handsome, usually well-behaved and she loved him deeply. She took the notice hanging on the doorknob of the room, added one letter with her pen and hung it on the outside of the door. The notice now read: 'Please Make Up Groom.'

❀

HOSPITALS

418. There was a loud scream from behind the curtains surrounding one of the beds in a hospital ward. A doctor rushed to the scene, pulled back the curtains and saw a trainee nurse with a kettle of hot water. A male patient was screaming and holding his crotch. Taking in the situation, the doctor snapped at the nurse: 'I think you mixed up your instructions. I believe you were asked to *prick* his *boil*.'

❂

419. As he wandered along the hospital corridors he suddenly heard a man say: 'We'll tak a cup o'kindness yet, for auld lang syne.'

He walked towards the voice and entered a large room where a woman said:

'Gin a body meet a body
Coming through the rye;
Gin a body kiss a body,
Need a body cry?'

As a student of literature he realised he was now in the Burns Unit.

❂

420. Medical operations generally only take a few hours to perform – but the people operated on can spend many evenings at dinner parties describing them.

❂

421. When herpes left the hospital it went on crotches.

❂

422. A man is seriously ill in hospital and his wife and five children visit him. They tell him how much they love him and, after wishing him well with his operation, the children leave the ward so he can talk privately with their mother.

'Darling,' said the man, 'you and the children all think I'm having an operation. But the surgeon told me today my condition has got worse. There are too many complications and I may not survive the night.'

The man's wife burst into tears as he continued: 'There is one thing I've always been unsure of and I hope you will answer honestly. All our children have dark hair, like you and me, except for the youngest, who has light brown hair. I can understand if he's not mine and you had a brief affair. I forgive you. But is he mine?'

'Yes,' replied the wife. 'I can honestly tell you he really is your son.'

Her husband smiled and lapsed into unconsciousness. His wife softly muttered to herself: 'Thank goodness he didn't ask me about the other four . . .'

❂

423. The elderly woman was in a hospital bed. She was about to have a serious operation and her husband was trying to comfort her, holding her hand and making soothing comments about their long life together.

'Yes, dear,' said the elderly woman. 'You were with me during the War when the bomb fell and destroyed our house, and I was trapped under the rubble for days and had to have my leg amputated before I could be freed. I also remember how you helped me start a business that we spent years building up before it went bankrupt and we lost everything. And then there was that time when we were together travelling in a bus which crashed into a wall, and I broke three ribs. Darling, *please* get out of the hospital *now* – you bring me bad luck!'

❂

424. One of the patients in the hospital was petrified about having an operation. 'Don't worry,' soothed a nurse. 'Your surgeon is one of the best in his field. He's performed thousands of operations – and hasn't cut himself once.'

❂

HOTELS
425. The bellboy knocked on Claude's hotel room door. 'Your suitcases, sir,' said the bellboy, wheeling them into the room.

After he had arranged the suitcases, the bellboy asked: 'Is there anything else I can get you, sir?'

'No thanks,' said Claude, giving the bellboy a tip.

The bellboy heard sounds of water splashing in the bathroom and saw a lady's dress lying on the bed.

'Perhaps your wife might like something?' suggested the bellboy.

'Oh!' said Claude. 'I almost forgot. Can you get me a postcard to send to her?'

☺

426. I recently stayed in such a cheap hotel that the staff stole towels from the guests.

☺

HOUSES
427. The middle-aged businessman returned from honeymoon with his young wife and showed her around his country house, telling her she could make whatever changes she liked: change the furniture, the wall coverings, and do a complete re-design of the entire house – whatever would make her happy.

A few days later the businessman had to return to his City office and apartment. His young wife soon set about making changes to the country house.

That weekend, when the businessman returned home, his wife embraced him and said she had prepared his dinner.

'I'll just get a bottle of wine from the cellar,' said the businessman. But when he entered the cellar he was shocked. Row after row of wine racks were completely empty. He could only find a few bottles of non-vintage wine.

'Darling,' called the businessman, 'where have you put the rest of the wine?'

'I had a major clear out,' replied his young wife. 'You had some really old bottles. Didn't you read the labels? It's not healthy to keep out-of-date stuff so I threw away all the wine that was past the date written on it.'

☺

428. I once bought a house in the country. By the time I finished paying for it, it was in town.

☺

HUNTING
429. It was in the days of the old American Wild West. A party of Englishmen had arrived in the US and wanted

to shoot some buffalo. They hired a guide who said he had been taught tracking and hunting techniques by the Indians.

After a long trek on horseback, without seeing any buffalo, the guide got off his horse. He bent down and put his ear to the ground. Then he said to the Englishmen: 'Buffalo have come this way.'

'How do you know?' asked one of the Englishmen. 'Does the ground vibrate with the sound of their approach?'

'No,' replied the guide. 'My ear is stuck in warm buffalo dung.'

❦

430. James and Keith went on a hunting holiday. On their second day they were walking in the woods when they suddenly realised they were lost. They sat and thought about their predicament.

Keith said: 'I remember from my granddad that the best way to get someone to come and rescue you is to fire three times in the air.'

'Good idea,' said James, and fired three times.

Thirty minutes later, there were no sounds of any rescuers so James fired again. Still no sounds of rescue.

After a further thirty minutes they fired three more times and Keith said: 'I hope a guide or some rescuers come soon – we've only got three more arrows left.'

❦

HUSBANDS

431. My husband has solutions to every problem. For example, he says the easiest way to remove red wine stains from a white silk dress is with a pair of scissors.

❦

432. My neighbour is lucky. Her husband uses paint that doesn't drip to decorate the house, whereas I'm married to a drip who doesn't paint.

❦

433. My husband has one thing that the more I stroke the bigger it gets – his ego.

❀

434. My husband is wonderful. He always remembers my birthday – but kindly forgets my age.

❀

435. When my husband was a small boy, he collected postage stamps. In his teens he collected women. In his twenties he collected cars – and then it was collections of antiques and fine wine. Now he's eighty he's still collecting – dust.

❀

436. What can a wife say to her husband just after they've made love?

Anything she likes as he's fast asleep.

❀

437. When I'm in bed with my husband I find that one good turn can get all the blankets.

❀

438. Last night my husband saw a horror film that scared him half to death. He's now worried in case he sees another one.

❀

439. Whenever my husband has to fill in a form giving details of 'person to notify in case of accident', he always writes: 'The nearest doctor.'

❀

440. When Helga paid an unexpected visit on her friend, Martha, she found Martha in a rather flustered state.

'I've just buried my husband,' explained Martha.

'Oh dear,' said Helga. 'But what happened to your clothes – they're all torn. And your hands and face are badly scratched.'

'I know,' replied Martha. 'It wasn't easy to bury him. Even after I hit him on the head with a spade he fought like mad.'

❀

441. My husband thinks that an IQ test is a lot of people being asked difficult questions while they stand in line outside an opticians.

❀

442. My husband is a light eater – as soon as it's light he starts eating.

❀

443. In a fight, some people use their fists. My husband uses his feet – he runs away as fast as possible.

❀

444. She came home from work to find her rather naïve husband wearing her raincoat underneath his overcoat – and he was painting the lounge.

'Why are you dressed like that to do some decorating?' she asked.

'I'm just following the direction on the paint tin,' he replied. 'For best results, put on two coats.'

❀

445. My husband keeps a record of everything he eats – it's on his tie.

❀

446. His mistress has the same first name as his wife. This was a deliberate safety measure on his part – in case he talks in his sleep.

❀

447. Miranda's husband is not a very good lover. He refused to look at the sex manual she bought him for Christmas, so his knowledge about loving remained minimal. Last week, when Miranda asked if they could try mutual orgasm, he said he was quite happy with their existing insurance company, Mutual Life.

❀

448. When his wife asked him why he kept coming home half drunk he replied that he never had enough money to get completely drunk.

❀

449. When Mavis was warned by her doctor not to touch anything alcoholic she told her husband not to go anywhere near her.

❀

450. My husband is so stupid that when he wants to count to eleven he has to unzip his fly.

✿

451. I wouldn't say he's hen-pecked – just spouse-broken.

✿

452. Wendy was sobbing as she phoned her best friend, Louise. 'It's my husband,' cried Wendy. 'He's just died.'

'Oh, I'm terribly sorry,' said Louise. 'Were you with him when he died?'

'Yes,' sobbed Wendy. 'I don't know what to do.'

'It must be terrible for you,' said Louise. 'Did he have any last requests?'

'Yes,' sobbed Wendy. 'He looked at me and asked: 'Please put down that gun. Please don't shoot me . . .'

✿

453. My husband used to have an unusual hobby. He collected train spotters until he had to give it up after developing anorakophobia.

✿

454. He's so stupid that whenever he paints the house his wife has to take precautions to stop him from hurting himself. She puts a 'Stop' sign on the top rung of his ladder.

✿

455. When I asked her how much her husband spent each week on beer, wine and spirits she replied: 'I don't exactly know, but looking at him, it must be a *staggering* amount.'

✿

456. My husband is a plastic surgeon. He performs operations to mend broken beaks on plastic ducks.

✿

457. He likes to help his wife with the housework – he lifts his legs up on to the sofa when she wants to vacuum the carpet.

✿

458. Her husband is a transvestite. He likes to eat, drink and be Mary.

✿

459. My husband keeps saying he's suffering from hallucinations – but I'm sure he's just imagining it.

460. My husband used to run a flea circus. He started it from scratch.

HYPNOTIST
461. The nymphomaniac was tired of sleeping around and being called unkind names so she went to a hypnotist and asked for his help. He soon solved her problem: it was a triumph of mind over mattress.

I

INNOCENCE
462. Some people can be so innocent – like the nuns who worked in a condom factory thinking they were making waterproof sleeping bags for mice.

❁

INTERNET
463. He knew he was addicted to the internet when he banged on the bathroom door and told his wife he urgently needed the toilet as he wanted to download.

❁

464. When I asked him if he had a website he replied: 'Yes. It's in a corner up on the ceiling of the lounge.'

❁

465. He's so naïve that when he heard a radio announcer mentioning a website address that included a 'forward slash' he thought it was a site devoted to urinating.

❁

INVENTORS
466. I've just been talking to an inventor who is trying to raise money for his new spray to help people get rid of flies and mosquitoes. He says it works twice as fast as some other methods. The spray is a specially formulated insect aphrodisiac. If you spray one insect with it another one will soon swoop down so you can swat the two of them together.

❁

J

JOBS

467. When I asked him why he had been fired from his job with an estate agency he said it was because his bosses discovered he was honest.

468. The girl was seated in the reception area of a large office, waiting with a number of other applicants to be interviewed for a job as personal assistant to the marketing director. She noticed that the other women were wearing smart suits and were busy re-reading their lengthy CVs. She felt rather out-of-place: she was rather busty and was dressed in a mini-skirt and a top with a plunging neckline and her CV amounted to no more than half a page.

At last it was her turn to be interviewed. After a few brief questions, the marketing director said: 'If I give you the job you'd be expected to do the same sort of thing you did in your previous job.'

'That's OK,' replied the busty girl, 'but could we do it on the sofa rather than on the desk?'

469. Last night he rushed home and told his wife: 'I've just found a fantastic job. Excellent pay, good holidays and excellent prospects. But hard work is expected.'

'Wonderful,' said his wife.

'Yes,' said the man. 'You start next week.'

470. Somehow I don't think he'll be offered the job for which he has applied. At the bottom of the application form, where it stated; 'Sign here' he wrote 'Capricorn'.

471. Last week my son started his first job after leaving university. This good news isn't really so great since he graduated ten years ago.

❁

L

LANGUAGES
472. When he went to work in the Far East he managed to learn Thai in five easy liaisons.

⊕

LAST WORDS
473. One angel's hobby was compiling a list of people's last words. His favourites included: 'Pull the pin out and count to *what*?', 'Which wire was I supposed to cut?' and 'There's no need to worry. These are the types of wild mushrooms it's perfectly safe to eat.'

⊕

LAW AND LAWYERS
474. The lawyer for the defence was cross-examining a witness.

'Now,' said the lawyer, 'you claim that my client bit a large chunk out of the victim's ear. Did you *see* him do it?'

'No,' replied the witness.

The lawyer smiled smugly and sneeringly asked: 'Then *how* can you *possibly* say that my client did it?'

'Easy,' replied the witness. 'I saw him spit out most of the ear.'

⊕

475. Lawyers believe that the best thing in life are fees.

⊕

476. The only thing a lawyer helps you with is to get what's coming to him.

⊕

477. A bank clerk was arrested and accused of embezzling millions from the bank. Lawyers from many law firms rushed to see him – but when he made his first appearance in court no lawyer could be found to act in his defence. He had proved to the lawyers that he was innocent and had no money.

❀

478. The prosecution lawyer was about to begin his questioning of one of the witnesses, a middle-aged man. 'Have you ever been cross-examined before?' asked the lawyer.

'Of course,' replied the witness. 'My wife is always cross when she questions me.'

❀

479. Lawyers don't *give* bad advice – they *charge* for it.

❀

480. Anyone who says talk is cheap hasn't employed a lawyer.

❀

481. If there's a lawyer involved, then where there's a will there's a delay.

❀

482. The senior partner in the law firm impressed upon the new recruits that bad lawyers can let a case drag on for six months. Good lawyers can earn a fat bonus by making the case last at least three times as long.

❀

LIFE
483. After a lot of study he's come to the conclusion that life is a sexually transmitted disease.

❀

484. He started out in life with nothing. He still has most of it.

❀

485. She used to have a handle on life – but it broke.

❀

LOSERS
486. He admires good losers – especially women who play strip poker.

❀

M

MAIL

487. If the world is getting smaller, why does it keep costing more money to send mail overseas?

❋

488. Nowadays, it's not people who send poison pen letters that you have to worry about – but those obnoxious people who make disgusting comments via the internet. Indeed, the e-mail of the species is deadlier than the mail.

❋

489. Old mailmen never die – they just get another posting.

❋

490. It has been said that people usually get what's coming to them – but I wonder if that's really true if it's been posted.

❋

MANAGEMENT CONSULTANTS

491. The rebels had moved into the holiday resort and captured three men: a management consultant and two salesmen.

The captives were taken to the rebel headquarters where they were to be held hostage until the government gave in to their demands.

Unfortunately, the government refused to comply with the rebels' requests so the three men were told they would be executed, but they could choose the method: firing squad or guillotine.

All three chose the guillotine, believing it would be the fastest and most painless end. Many members of the rebel army seemed to be hooked on drugs and the firing squad's aim might not be too accurate and the captured men might just be badly injured and slowly bleed to death.

The first salesman was brought to the guillotine. He knelt down with his head in the correct position – and the blade came down – but stopped before it could cut his neck.

'This is a sign from God,' said the salesman. 'He does not want me to be killed. You should set me free.' He then went on in great detail about how he would promote the rebels' cause to the outside world. The rebel leader agreed to let him go.

One of the rebels re-adjusted the guillotine and the second salesman was forced into position. The blade came hurtling down – but stopped before it reached him.

'Another sign from God,' shouted the salesman. 'You should free me. Not only will I promote your cause I can raise money for you, too.'

The rebel leader agreed to let him go.

Then the management consultant was led towards the guillotine, but he shouted: 'Stop! That thing clearly does not work properly. You'd better use the firing squad instead.'

❂

492. If you're at a cocktail party and you suspect one of the guests is a management consultant, just go up to him and ask: 'Can you tell me the time?'

If he asks to borrow your watch, then he's a management consultant.

❂

MARRIAGE AND MARRIED LIFE

493. Although a romantic young couple's billing and cooing may lead to marriage – they should remember that the billing never ends.

❂

494. When I asked him how he had got a large bruise on his cheek, he told me it was caused by a glancing blow. He had been out shopping with his wife when he had glanced at a beautiful woman. His wife hit him.

❂

495. We've been married ten years and never a cross word – my wife cuts them out of the newspaper so I can never do them.

☺

496. Nigel was distraught. He had received an anonymous phone call at his office, telling him that his wife was having an affair with a man who worked for a pest control company.

Nigel rushed home to discover a pest control van in his driveway. He let himself into the house. There was no sign of his wife. Then he walked up the stairs and heard sounds of feverish activity.

Flinging open the bedroom door he saw his wife zipping up her dress.

'You're home early, dear,' said his wife. 'I was just putting on some clean clothes. The others got messed up when I was showing the pest control man the attic.'

'Where is he now?' asked Nigel.

'I'm not too sure,' replied the wife.

Nigel looked around the bedroom and opened a cupboard. Standing inside was a naked man.

'What is the meaning of this?' demanded Nigel.

'Well,' replied the naked man. 'After looking for woodworm in the loft I thought there might be an infestation of moths in the bedroom.'

'Where are your clothes?' asked Nigel.

The naked man looked down at himself, appeared to be astonished, and exclaimed: 'Those blasted moths must have eaten them!'

☺

497. When men get married it's usually because they have been *miss*-led.

☺

498. Roland told his father: 'I'm going to get married. I've found a woman just like mum.'

'Oh,' said the father. 'Do you want congratulations or commiserations?'

☺

499. At the start of their marriage they were not deeply in love, but over the years he developed a great attachment for his wife – it fitted over her mouth.

❂

500. He recently asked his wife: 'What have you been doing with all the grocery money I give you?'

She replied: 'Stand sideways and look in the mirror.'

❂

501. The hen-pecked husband could stand it no more. 'I'm off to join the Foreign Legion,' he said to his wife as he packed a suitcase.

His wife looked at him with a sneer and said: 'Well, when you get back make sure you take off your shoes before coming into the house. I don't want sandy footprints all over the carpet!'

❂

502. When Robert came home unexpectedly early from work one day he found his wife in bed with another man.

'How dare you!' shouted Robert at his wife. 'Who *is* this man?'

Robert's wife replied. 'We only met at lunchtime. I forgot to ask his name.'

❂

503. They have been married for twenty-five years – and they are still in love: he with his secretary, and she with the gardener.

❂

504. People who have been married for a very long time usually continue to remain married. This proves that people who *grey* together, stay together.

❂

505. My wife lets me run things around the house – the washing machine, vacuum cleaner and dishwasher.

❂

506. She married a dreamboat – but he soon turned into a destroyer.

❂

507. His marriage is based on trust and understanding. She doesn't trust him – and he can't understand her.

❂

508. When Sally came home from work her husband said: 'Let's go out and have some fun tonight.'

'Good idea,' replied Sally. 'But if you get home before I do, remember not to put the chain on the front door.'

✿

509. When his wife asked him why he drank so much he replied: 'I'm hoping to escape hearing all your nagging by getting *liquor* mortis.'

✿

510. It is often said that when a man and a woman marry they become one. But no one asks 'one what?' – so some couples can spend years arguing over which one or what.

✿

511. If it is true that love is blind – then marriage is certainly an eye-opener.

✿

512. She's a 'husband seismologist' – always looking at her husband trying to find faults.

✿

513. My wife believes in an open marriage – she opens my mail, and my wallet.

✿

514. He was so hen-pecked that when, at last, he managed to interrupt his wife to make a comment, she snapped: 'Be quiet! When I want your opinion, I'll give it to you.'

✿

515. Their marriage broke up because he was always leaving the house after shouting a four letter word at his wife: 'Golf' or 'Work'.

✿

516. His son asked him: 'How much does it cost to get married?' He replied: 'I don't really know – I'm still paying for it.'

✿

517. There are only two times in a man's life when he won't be able to understand women – the time when he's single and the time when he's married.

✿

518. Last night he decided to cheer himself up. He turned on the TV, put the video of his wedding day in the video machine – and played the video backwards. He smiled as he saw himself walk out of the church as a single man.

☻

519. There are a lot of pathetic jokes in the world. I should know – I married one of them.

☻

520. When John made his girlfriend pregnant her father sent two large, powerful men to his office to discuss John's marriage – it was a wife or death situation.

☻

521. My brother-in-law broke up my marriage – my husband came home early one day and found me in bed with him.

☻

522. David's wife was in tears. 'What's wrong?' he asked.

'It's our daughter Fiona,' sobbed the wife. 'I know she's in love with Mike and they'll make a lovely couple. But she's only twenty and when she marries she'll leave home and . . .'

'There, there,' soothed David. 'I know we'll be losing a daughter but we'll be gaining a bathroom and a telephone.'

☻

523. She got all excited about nothing – and then married him.

☻

524. Susan's marriage to Simon had fallen on rocky times. They had married young and Susan had soon become bored.

On Friday night Simon was appalled when his wife staggered home drunk.

'You've been out partying with that slimy boss of yours,' shouted Simon.

'No I haven't,' said Susan.

'This is the third time this week you've come home drunk. I demand to know what's going on – especially as you've got what looks like a love bite on your neck. Who is it you've been seeing? I demand to know!'

Susan remained silent.

'Is it Paul from the local taxi firm? I've never liked the way he leers at you whenever we get in his cab? Or is it that shoe shop man? Last week he looked at you almost longingly and stroked your feet while you chose some shoes? Or is it cousin Tom? Whenever we meet him he's forever rubbing your shoulders and offering you a neck massage.'

'It's none of them,' said Susan as she staggered up the stairs to bed. 'But thank you for giving me some leads for further romance.'

❂

525. When I was single I used to *yearn* for a woman to love. Now I've got one I need to *earn* for her.

❂

526. The reason he married someone so much shorter than himself is because it was the only way he could be sure at least someone would look up to him.

❂

527. She married a man from Czechoslovakia so she could be sure of getting something long and hard – his surname.

❂

528. Before they married he told his wife-to-be that he would climb the highest mountain, swim the largest ocean and trek across the North Pole for her. After two years of marriage she divorced him because he was always away from home.

❂

529. My husband asked if we could try a different position tonight. I said: certainly! He could stand in the kitchen making dinner, while I sat on the sofa watching TV.

❂

530. During an argument his wife snapped: '*Why* did I have to marry you to discover exactly how stupid you are?'

He replied: 'You didn't have to do that. You should have known immediately I *asked* you to marry me.'

❂

531. The secret of their long and happy marriage is that three times a week they go out for a romantic meal – he with his mistress, and she with her lover.

☺

532. After five years of marriage he could not stand his wife any more. He hated her bad temper and the way she hissed and spat at him – so he ran away and joined the Foreign Legion. Unfortunately, out in the desert the camels looked and acted just like his wife.

☺

533. Claude and his wife were having an argument over the solution to a crossword clue.

'I *know* my answer is right,' said Claude. 'I'm not a *complete* idiot!'

'Really?' sneered his wife. 'Which part of you is missing?'

☺

534. Uncle Clive is my *dearest* relative. He's been married eight times – and each time I've had to buy him a wedding present.

☺

MARRIAGE PROPOSAL
535. Melissa and David were kissing and cuddling on the sofa and, as their passion increased, David said: 'My little peach. You are the apple of my eye. Will you marry me?'

Melissa kissed him deeply and said: 'Of course, my little plum.'

Then Melissa's small brother, who had been hiding behind the sofa, said: 'And I now pronounce you a fruit salad.'

☺

MEDICAL STUDENTS
536. The young male medical student was so excited and happy he shouted 'Hooray!' when he was assigned to the maternity ward.

'Why so happy?' asked a young nurse.

'Well,' replied the medical student, 'when I was in Ear, Nose and Throat I kept imagining I had all sorts of problems with my ears and nose. Then I wondered if I had tonsillitis. Then I was assigned to Urology – and kept imagining I had all sorts of urinary problems. But now I get to be in maternity and I'm so happy. I don't think I'll be imagining I'm giving birth.'

❂

537. One of the medical students has a lot of studying to do. He still thinks that varicose veins are veins that are too close together.

❂

538. The medical students were studying anatomy. Their professor stood facing the students. He had a naked male cadaver laid out in front of him.

Turning the male body over so that its buttocks were facing him, the professor said: 'There are two important things you *must* remember.'

He inserted his finger into the dead man's anus, then pulled out the finger and said: 'The first thing is that you should not be afraid to perform what may seem to be disgusting tasks.'

The professor held his finger under his nose, sniffed, then touched it with his tongue before wiping the finger clean.

'Now,' said the professor, 'I want you all to do the same.'

With some trepidation, the students lined up and each inserted a finger into the dead man's anus, took out the finger, held it under their nose, sniffed the finger and then touched it with their tongue before wiping their finger clean.

When they had each completed the task, the professor looked at them and shook his head sadly. 'The second thing you have to remember,' said the professor, 'is to be very observant. I hope you will do better in future – but today you all failed. I watched you all closely – and each of you sniffed and touched with your tongue your finger that had been in the cadaver's anus. But if you had been really observing me closely you would have noticed that the finger I sniffed and touched with my tongue was a different finger from the one I put in the cadaver.'

❁

539. The young medical student said that he eventually wanted to specialise in gynaecology because he knew it had lots of interesting openings.

❁

540. When the very new medical student asked the nurse for advice on how he could tell the difference between a rectal and an oral thermometer she replied: 'Taste.'

❁

MEN

541. Although she believes that all men are animals she's discovered that some make quite good pets.

❁

542. The main difference between men and women is that the average woman wants *one* man to satisfy *all* her needs, while the average man wants *all* women to satisfy his *one* need.

❁

543. Last night she had a man in her bed gasping for breath and calling her name. She was trying to smother her husband with a pillow.

❁

544. He's an incredible man. He doesn't know the meaning of fear, defeat or surrender – so I've bought him a dictionary.

❁

545. Why do men become smarter when they are having sex with a woman?

Because at that time they are plugged into a genius.

❁

546. Some women have discovered that men are rather like carpets – lay them well and it's easier to walk all over them.

❁

547. How can you tell if a man is well hung?

When there's no sign of movement from him and you can't put your finger between his neck and the rope around it.

☸

548. Why do men have larger brains than dogs?

So they won't try and hump women's legs at cocktail parties.

☸

549. Why were men created with their sex organ hanging on the outside of their body?

So it would be easier for them to find it.

☸

550. She says that it is impossible for men to get mad cow disease as all men are pigs.

☸

551. What is the difference between government bonds and men?

Bonds mature.

☸

552. After years of careful study, women have concluded that the easiest time to change a male is when he's a baby.

☸

553. Women are so unkind these days. I heard one ask: 'What is that useless piece of skin called on the end of a penis?' and her friend replied: 'A man.'

☸

554. She believes that men are rather like photocopiers. Apart from being needed for reproduction, what else are they good for?

☸

555. How can you make 2.5 kilograms of female fat attractive to a man?

Stick a nipple on it.

☸

556. What do you call a man with 75 per cent of his brain missing?

Castrated.

☸

557. She thinks that men are rather like very old cars. They are difficult to get started, they emit noxious odours, and a lot of the time they don't work.

✿

558. When he finally managed to get his head together, his body started to fall apart.

✿

559. Some women find that men are a bit like high heels – once you practise a bit they are easy to walk on.

✿

560. All men are beasts – so it's a good job I love animals . . .

✿

MICE
561. Three male mice were chatting and the conversation turned to courage and strength.

'I'm so tough,' said the first mouse, 'that I can take cheese from a mouse trap by holding back the metal spring.'

'So what,' said the second mouse. 'My body is so strong that I can eat rat poison and it has no effect.'

'Oh well,' said the third mouse. 'I can't stay here talking – I have to get home in time to have sex with the cat.'

✿

562. Why do mice have small balls?

Because not very many of them know how to dance.

✿

MILITARY
563. When he was an officer in the army his men would follow him anywhere – mainly out of curiosity.

✿

564. Soon after he joined the army he was put on sentry duty. It was obvious to everyone that he was a new recruit since he challenged each person who tried to enter the camp by saying: 'Halt! Who goes there? Goody or Baddy?'

✿

565. My husband's in the army. He keeps being posted abroad and I hardly ever see him. In fact, I'm worried I won't recognise him when he turns up on the doorstep expecting a romantic welcome. That's why I have to kiss passionately every man who comes to the door.

❁

566. The new recruit to the army was keen to learn as much as possible about army life. At every opportunity he questioned his longer-serving comrades. This constant barrage of questions got on their nerves so when he asked: 'If I accidentally step on a landmine, what should I do?' one of them responded: 'Well, usually, people leap into the air and scatter themselves over the area.'

❁

567. The armies of three nations were involved in a military exercise. '*My* soldiers are the bravest,' said the commander of a large country's army. Of course, the commanders of the other nations disagreed.

To settle their dispute they each chose the soldier whom they thought was the bravest in their land.

The first soldier was ordered by his commander to strip naked and fight, unarmed, ten soldiers in uniform. He immediately did as he was commanded and although he managed to overpower three of the soldiers he was eventually beaten unconscious, suffering broken ribs, legs and a broken nose.

'See,' said his commander. 'That's real bravery. Despite unbeatable odds of ten-to-one he still went ahead without fear or hesitation.'

The second nation's commander ordered his chosen soldier to strip naked and fight twenty soldiers in uniform. At the end of the fight, as the man lay dying on the ground, his commander said: 'That's true bravery. He managed to defeat five soldiers and not only showed no fear, but was proud to die for his country's honour.'

The third nation's commander ordered his chosen soldier to strip naked and fight a whole platoon. 'Strip naked?' queried the soldier. 'Are you some sort of pervert? And fight a whole platoon? No, you're completely mad and I won't do it.'

His commander smiled and told the other commanders: 'Now *that* is genuine bravery.'

❀

MONEY

568. If money talks, then why does so much of it seem to say 'goodbye'?

❀

569. Money can't buy love. But it *can* hire a good imitation.

❀

570. The only reason he is richer than me is because he's got more money.

❀

MORNINGS

571. I'm not very good in the morning until after I've had breakfast. For example, when I got up this morning I staggered to the bathroom, stared in the mirror and wondered where I'd seen that face before.

❀

572. When people wake up in the morning they usually rub or scratch the part of the body nearest their brain. That's why women rub their forehead and eyes and men scratch their balls.

❀

MOSQUITOES

573. The world would have been a much better place if Noah had refused to let the two mosquitoes board the Ark.

❀

MUSIC AND SINGERS

574. The thing that puzzles me most about rap music is why they spell 'rap' without the initial 'c'.

❀

575. The young pop singer was puzzled. His mother had told him not to let success go to his head. He should remember to keep his feet firmly on the ground. He wondered how he could do that and still put on his trousers or sleep in a bed.

❀

576. The famous rock star went to a doctor and admitted that he was suffering from impotence.

'Are you sure?' asked the doctor. 'According to the press you've got a wonderful reputation with women.'

The rock star sighed and said: 'That's just a reputation – but it won't stand up.'

❁

N

NAMES

577. One day, when someone struggles to remember a person's name and says: 'What's his name? I know it. Now what is it? It's on the tip of my tongue.' I might have the courage to reply: 'Mr Spit.'

☺

578. He wanted to be a household name – so he changed his name to Hoover.

☺

579. Four men were sitting in a bar at an airport waiting for their flights to be called. 'I'm keen to get home,' said one of the men. 'Tomorrow is St George's Day and it's my eldest son's birthday. We named him George as it seemed the most suitable name.'

'What a coincidence,' said another of the men. 'My son was born on St Patrick's Day and we named him Patrick.'

'Incredible!' said the third man. 'My son was born on St Andrew's Day and we named him Andrew.'

'What's even more amazing,' said the fourth man, 'is that my son was also named for the day of his birth: Pancake.'

☺

580. He asked if he could call her later. She said she'd prefer it if he called her Caroline.

☺

581. He can only remember the names of people less than five feet two inches tall – he has a short memory.

☺

NEIGHBOURS

582. If you want to love your neighbour then it's best to make sure their spouse is away when you do it.

☺

583. Instead of spending lots of money trying to keep *up* with the neighbours or your work colleagues try, instead, to bring them *down* to your level.

❂

NEUTRONS
584. I was drinking at a bar last night. I got chatting to the barmaid who told me she was working in the bar three evenings a week in order to help support herself at university where she was studying physics. As we were talking, a neutron walked in and asked her: 'How much for a gin and tonic?'

The barmaid looked at the neutron and said: 'For you, no charge.'

❂

O

OFFICE LIFE

585. The office junior was keen to make a good impression. Her boss asked her to get him a cup of coffee from the shop on the corner of the street – but he stressed that he did not want it in a plastic or paper cup – he wanted it in a ceramic cup.

The office junior eagerly agreed, walked down the two flights of stairs to the street, opened the door, and walked a hundred yards to the coffee shop, then back to the office. She presented her boss with his coffee – filled to the brim of the cup.

'That's great!' said the boss, and the office junior smiled with pleasure.

This went on twice a day for several weeks until one of the office junior's colleagues became curious.

'I'm amazed,' said the colleague. 'How do you manage to walk a hundred yards back from the coffee shop every day, dodging pedestrians on a busy street, and then walk up two flights of stairs and give the boss his cup of coffee filled right to the brim. There is no lid to the cup – so how can you do it without spilling any coffee?'

'Don't tell the boss,' said the office junior, 'but before I leave the coffee shop I take a big sip of the coffee and hold it in my mouth until I get just outside the office door – and then I spit it back into the cup.'

❀

586. He was telling his wife how good his colleague was at the office. 'He's so helpful – I'd trust him with my life.'

'But,' she said, 'would you trust him with anything of great value?'

❀

587. He likes to do things right the first time. But he deliberately doesn't do it too often. He says he wants people to realise fully that his work is very difficult.

❀

588. He didn't go to work yesterday because he was sick. He was sick of work.

❀

589. There's a man in my office whose nickname is Caterpillar – because he's always crawling.

❀

590. She made a complete mess of the office accounts, but managed to get sympathy from her boss when she followed her motto: If at first you don't succeed then cry, cry and cry again.

❀

591. When a man talks dirty to a woman in his office it's sexual harassment. When a woman talks dirty to a man in his office it costs a fortune in premium rate phone calls.

❀

592. She used to file her nails in the office – in the large grey filing cabinet under 'N'.

❀

593. Trains stop at a train station. Buses stop at a bus station. So why should I act differently in the office at my work station?

❀

594. He believes: If at first you don't succeed – then find someone to blame it on.

❀

595. As Andrew, a handsome young man, was rushing to pack his briefcase ready to leave the office, an attractive young woman came over to his desk. She smiled at him and said: 'T.G.I.F.'

Andrew stopped and looked at her. She smiled again and said: 'T.G.I.F.'

Andrew muttered 'S.H.I.T. and continued his frantic packing.

The young woman looked at him longingly and said:
'T.G.I.F. – Thank Goodness It's Friday.'
'S.H.I.T.' said Andrew. 'Sorry Honey, It's Thursday.'
✿

P

PARROTS

596. Tom was very annoyed with his parrot. Every time someone visited Tom's home, the parrot would say something offensive.

Tom tried to make the parrot behave. When the parrot shouted 'Fat cow, fat cow' at Tom's mother, Tom flicked cold water at his pet.

When the parrot shouted obscene four-letter words at a visiting priest, Tom hastily covered the parrot's cage and kept the bird in the dark for a whole day.

The final straw came when the parrot made such disgusting comments to Tom's girlfriend that she stormed out of the house. Tom scolded the bird, took it out of its cage, put it in a strong transparent plastic box with air holes, and put it in the freezer. He told the bird: 'It's time you cooled down.'

Ten minutes later, Tom opened the freezer, and the parrot said: 'Sorry! Sorry! I've learnt my lesson. I'll behave. But please let me know what the chicken in here said to annoy you . . .'

❀

597. Why did the parrot wear a plastic raincoat?

Because it was starting to rain heavily so it wanted to be polyunsaturated.

❀

PICNICS

598. If ants are always supposed to be so busy – how is it that they can spend so much time at picnics?

❀

599. Although he has terrible body odour we still take him with us on picnics in the summer. His smell helps to keep the flies away from the food.

❀

PLANE TRAVEL

600. When he fell asleep on the plane and suddenly awoke, trembling and panic-stricken from a horrible nightmare, he quickly pressed the call button for the *fright* attendant.

❀

601. Gerald was flying solo in a small plane across Africa when suddenly he noticed the fuel gauge was registering 'empty'. The engine started to make spluttering noises and it seemed clear that the plane had a leak in its fuel tanks.

Hastily putting on a parachute, Gerald jumped out of the plane and landed in a small clearing in the jungle. He was soon surrounded by a group of large men carrying spears and making threatening noises.

'I mean no harm,' said Gerald.

'He speak English,' said a tall, thin man pushing his way in front of the large men. 'I'm Henry,' said the thin man. 'I've lived with this tribe for the past ten years, ever since I was on an expedition and fell in love with the chief's daughter.'

Gerald was delighted to meet Henry and they chatted happily about each other's adventures and how Gerald might find his way out of the jungle. While they were talking, the tribesmen were busily building a huge fire and preparing a feast.

'There is, however, a tradition amongst the tribe,' said Henry. 'Strangers have to prove they are worthy of being helped. Otherwise they are left to fend for themselves – and in this jungle you could well remain lost forever or die of hunger or be killed by wild animals.'

'How can I show I'm worthy?' asked Gerald.

'You have to perform three tasks,' replied Henry. 'The first is fairly simple. You just have to drink a bowl of their special drink – but I warn you it is extremely potent with a very high alcohol content.'

'That's OK,' said Gerald, and a bowl of green liquid was handed to him.

As he was drinking, Henry told him of the remaining tasks. The ugliest woman in the village was very unhappy because no one would have sex with her, so Gerald had to make love to her. The tribe's pet goat had an infected, bad tooth which Gerald had to remove.

Finishing the drink, Gerald was led to a hut where the goat lay moaning on the ground. Shutting the door, Gerald was left to complete his task. After five minutes, during which loud cries and moans came from the hut, Gerald staggered out through the door and said: 'Second task done. Now where is that ugly woman with a bad tooth?'

❀

602. The plane suddenly seemed to rock about and the captain turned on the public address system and said: 'There's nothing to worry about. It's just a mechanical problem. The two engines seem to have lost a bit of power and one of them is on fire – so I'm just putting on my parachute and going for help.'

❀

603. The plane went into a steep dive. The pilot announced: 'We have a problem. Stay calm and pray. We're doing all we can to fix things.'

The plane then began to come out of the dive, but then jolted and shuddered, and passengers could see that one of the plane's engines was on fire.

'I can't die like this!' shouted a woman. 'I'm twenty-five and no man has ever made me feel like a *real* woman. I must have a *real* man *now*!'

A young man sitting behind her ripped off his shirt, displaying his rippling muscles and the woman sighed. Her pleas had brought her this gorgeous hunk.

'I can make you feel like a *real* woman,' he said as he handed her his shirt and said: 'Iron this.'

❀

604. I've just returned from a foreign holiday. On the journey home one of the stewardesses announced proudly:

'You may be interested to know that your entire crew today are women, so you are in especially capable, caring and safe hands. Even the pilot and co-pilot are women.'

A small boy put up his hand and asked: 'Can I visit the cockpit?'

A stewardess smiled and said: 'It's not called a cockpit any more.'

❂

POLICE AND DETECTIVES

605. Sherlock Holmes was in his study reading a newspaper. Watson entered and Sherlock looked up and said: 'I believe that you were in a hurry early this morning.'

'Yes,' replied Watson. 'How did you know that?'

'And,' said Sherlock, 'I deduce that you are wearing your pink-striped underpants.'

'My goodness!' said Watson. 'How do you know that?'

'Because,' replied Sherlock, 'you have forgotten to put your trousers on.'

❂

606. The detective had a good reputation for solving crimes – but this was because in all his cases people either left obvious clues or witnesses came forward to point out the criminals. That was why the detective's colleagues called him Sheer-Luck Holmes.

❂

607. She was stopped by the police for speeding. The police claimed she was travelling at over a hundred miles per hour. She denied the charge as she said she couldn't possibly have done that as she had only been driving for fifteen minutes.

❂

608. The young woman was forced to stop her car by the police. 'Didn't you see the thirty miles an hour sign?' asked a policeman.

'No,' replied the woman. 'I was driving too fast to see it.'

❂

609. When he was arrested in a foreign country he was pleased when he heard the chief of police tell him: 'You

will get a fair trial' – but wept when the police chief
continued: '. . . and then you will be shot.'

❂

POLITICIANS
610. What's a bore hole?
A politician's mouth.

❂

611. A political party had been rocked by bad publicity
surrounding the sexual exploits of a number of its members. The leader ordered all its elected members to attend a
meeting at which he encouraged them all to become
golfers.

'If you want rest and recreation, I urge you all to turn to
golf,' he said. 'You all know what happens if the press
catch you reading pornographic magazines or indulging in
sex with people to whom you are not married – but with
golf you can have lots of fun without the worry.'

'Yes,' said the deputy leader. 'The press don't mind you
reading golf magazines, playing a round with a stranger,
or even playing a round with a pro. And remember – you
also don't need to worry about golf-transmitted diseases.'

❂

612. What do you call an honest, intelligent politician?
Extinct.

❂

613. The politician attended a conference at a university
and insisted that academic standards had not fallen. After
his speech he went to one of the university toilets and saw,
printed on the wall above a roll of toilet paper: 'Political
studies degrees. Please take one.'

❂

614. Soon after the terrorists kidnapped six politicians
and fed them to the lions and tigers in a zoo, the terrorists
were captured, tried and sentenced to a long term in jail –
for cruelty to animals.

❂

615. Not all politicians should be shot – some should be
guillotined.

❂

616. Why does it take longer to build a snowman that looks like a politician than it does to build an ordinary snowman?

Because to be more realistic, you have to spend extra time hollowing out the head.

✿

617. The danger with political jokes is that sometimes they get elected.

✿

618. Politicians should be regularly changed for the same reason as nappies.

✿

619. There is no such thing as a 'cheap politician' – they actually cost a fortune.

✿

620. In countries where there are two main political parties there is sometimes little to tell them apart. Each of them will have corrupt politicians after your money – but one of them will probably have politicians who are also after your daughters.

✿

621. Different countries treat news of disasters in different ways. For example, suppose there was a large asteroid heading towards Earth. There is nothing that can be done to stop it and it will hit the Earth within seven days. When the asteroid hits the Earth it will kill everything on the planet.

In the USA the President would either keep quiet about the impending disaster, for fear of causing a panic, or would make a stately address to the nation urging people to pray and keep calm.

In some other countries the leaders would blame the rulers of nations they hate and would use it as an excuse to declare war on them.

In some countries the leaders would say that the asteroid did not exist or, if it did, it would not hit Earth. The disaster scenario was just a wicked foreign ploy to cause panic.

In a few countries the leaders would believe they were personally invincible and even if the asteroid hit Earth they would be saved. So they would hide in underground bunkers with a supply of food, water, air and trusted and nubile young men and women.

In Britain the Prime Minister would say: 'Within seven days no one in Britain will need to worry about problems on the trains or with the health service.'

✿

622. What do aliens and intelligent politicians have in common?

People talk about them but rarely see them – and some wonder if they exist at all.

✿

623. The politician told his wife that he needed to get more headlines in order to advance his career. His wife said she thought he had enough lines on his forehead already.

✿

POLYGAMY
624. One of the disadvantages of polygamy is the hours a husband must wait trying to get into the bathroom.

✿

PRESENTS
625. 'Darling', he said to his wife. 'What would you like for your birthday? A new car? A round-the-world holiday?'

'None of those things,' replied his wife. 'I want a divorce.'

'Oh!' he replied. 'I wasn't intending to spend that much.'

✿

626. His brother is a man of rare gifts – he rarely gives any.

✿

627. It was Christmas and Quentin decided to buy some perfume as a present for his wife.

At the perfume counter in a large department store, the assistant sprayed some perfume on his wrist. 'Smells quite nice,' said Quentin. But when the assistant told him the price, Quentin said: 'Far too expensive.'

The assistant let him sniff a sample of a much cheaper brand, but still Quentin said it was too expensive.

'You're nicely dressed,' said the sales assistant. 'Do you have a good job?'

'Yes,' replied Quentin.

'And is the perfume for your wife?' asked the assistant.

'Yes,' said Quentin. 'We've been married ten years. But the perfumes you've shown me so far are still much too expensive. Can you show me something really cheap?'

'I suggest,' replied the sales assistant, 'that you look in the mirror.'

❁

628. What do you give a man who has all the latest high-tech gadgets?

The services of a six-year-old boy to show him how to work them all.

❁

629. My wife wanted a new car – preferably a BMW or Jaguar – for her birthday but I'm giving her a ring with a large diamond in it instead. No one sells cheap fake BMWs or Jaguars.

❁

PRINCESS

630. She was a very promiscuous princess – she made every second count.

❁

PROVERBS AND SAYINGS

631. The severity of an itch increases in proportion to its distance from reachability.

❁

632. The man who gives in and apologises when he is wrong is wise. The man who gives in and apologises when he is right is married.

❁

633. It is better to be pissed *off* than pissed *on*.

❁

634. A closed mouth gathers no foot.

❀

635. When the chips are down – the fish or hamburger can't be far behind.

❀

636. Some of today's trash could be tomorrow's treasures.

❀

637. Taking the right fork in the road can avoid a knife in the back.

❀

638. Never eat yellow snow.

❀

639. It has been said that change is inevitable – except from a vending machine.

❀

640. The quickest way to find something is to buy a replacement for the thing you lost – then it will re-appear.

❀

641. Go to an orgy – try grope therapy.

❀

642. Never mention the number 288 in polite company – it's two gross.

❀

643. Impotence is just nature's way of saying 'no hard feelings'.

❀

644. A lack of curiosity kills the chat.

❀

645. A face can say so many things – especially the mouth part.

❀

646. If you can't find a solution to a problem, find someone to blame.

❀

647. It is best not to play leapfrog with a unicorn.

❀

648. If at first you don't succeed – then you probably shouldn't try skydiving.

❀

649. You've only got to look at popular sayings to know that it's true that women are more intelligent than men. For example, 'Diamonds are a girl's best friend' but 'A man's best friend is his dog.'

❂

PSYCHIATRIST
650. To make teenagers more comfortable when talking to him on his couch a psychiatrist I know gives them a mobile phone to hold.

❂

PSYCHIC
651. I've just been reading the job ads. in the newspaper. I was particularly impressed with the one that stated: 'Psychic wanted – you know what for and where to apply.'

❂

PUT-DOWNS
652. Is that snot hanging out of your nose – or is your brain leaking?

❂

653. He's as thick as a plank of wood. What you might think is dandruff on his shoulders is really sawdust.

❂

654. When he was born something really dreadful happened. He survived.

❂

655. He's a well-balanced person. He has a chip on both shoulders.

❂

656. The kindest thing you can say about her is that she's biodegradable.

❂

657. She still looks like she did twenty years ago – ugly and old.

❂

658. The two worst things about him are his face.

❂

659. He's got a good head on his shoulders – it's just a pity it's not on his neck.

❂

660. Thank you for your comments. They clearly demonstrate that you came from the shallow end of the gene pool.

❖

661. I'm fascinated by your appearance. Is that a head on your shoulders – or is it some mad scientist's experiment of growing hair on a meatball?

❖

662. He recently took an intelligence test. The results came back negative.

❖

663. When the man tried to argue with him, the conference speaker said: 'I'm sorry, but I don't want to enter into a battle of wits with someone who is only a half.'

❖

664. He's a real lady-killer – after one night with him they commit suicide.

❖

665. If I'm heckled during a speech one useful put down is to say to the heckler: 'You can go home now, your cage has been cleaned.'

❖

666. The difference between her and the Grand Old Duke of York is that the Duke only had ten thousand men.

❖

667. He's got something that makes women go crazy. Rabies.

❖

668. If you want to see something really funny, then look in a mirror.

❖

669. I wouldn't say she has a big mouth – but she puts her lipstick on with a paint-roller.

❖

670. If you want to know what sexual position creates the ugliest children – then ask your mother.

❖

671. Why are you wasting your breath asking me difficult questions? You'll need all your breath tonight in bed when you blow up your inflatable doll.

⚙

672. His problem is that he stopped to think – but then forgot to re-start.

⚙

Q

QUESTIONS

673. Why is it that bills seem to travel through the postal system at a much faster speed than cheques?

❁

674. What do you get if you cross an insomniac, an agnostic and a dyslexic?

Someone who lies awake at night wondering if there is a dog.

❁

675. When he was asked: 'What is the difference between ignorance and apathy?', he replied: 'I don't know – and I don't care!'

❁

676. What is longer than it is wide, has a head on it and pleases women?

Big denomination currency notes.

❁

677. What is the best thing to take when you are run down?

The registration number of the vehicle.

❁

678. If Santa Claus, an honest politician and a small boy are walking together along a street and simultaneously see a wallet on the ground, which of them picks up the wallet first?

The small boy. The other two don't really exist.

❁

679. What has balls and screws you every week?

The National Lottery.

❁

680. Why is the time when traffic goes the most slowly called the rush hour?

❁

681. Why is it that when you dial the wrong telephone number by mistake it's never engaged?

❄

682. What goes in hard and quite stiff and comes out soft and wet?
Chewing gum.

❄

683. What should you do if a bird makes a mess on your car?
Never go on a date with her again.

❄

684. What is the difference between a porcupine and a Porsche?
On the porcupine all the pricks are on the outside.

❄

685. When he told me that ignorance is bliss I asked him: 'Is that why you always look so blissful?'

❄

686. He looked rather ill so I asked him: 'How do you feel?'
He replied: 'With my hands.'

❄

687. What is quite big, hard and sticks out of a man's pyjamas so far that it is possible to hang a hat on it?
The man's head.

❄

688. Why is it that what something used to cost to buy, it now costs twice as much as that to repair?

❄

689. What is a zebra?
Much bigger than an A bra.

❄

690. What do the starship Enterprise and toilet paper have in common?
They have both visited Uranus looking for Klingons.

❄

691. The male professor of sociology asked a female colleague: 'Why is it that in most societies women try to impress the males with their looks, rather than their brains?'

'Simple!' replied his female colleague. 'Studies have shown that there is a far greater chance that a man is likely to be a moron than have problems with his eyesight.'

☻

QUESTIONS FOR KIDS

692. What is the favourite ride of ghosts at a fairground?
The roller-ghoster.

☻

693. Where do horrible creatures like to eat?
At a beastro.

☻

694. Where do you find the most fish?
Between the head and the tail.

☻

695. What do you call a bee that doesn't speak clearly?
A mumble bee.

☻

696. When the witch typed the manuscript of her book on her computer, which function on the computer did she like the most?
The spell checker.

☻

697. What bone has no appeal to a dog?
A trombone.

☻

698. What do you call a cat that likes eating lemons and drinking vinegar?
A sourpuss.

☻

699. Why do bananas never snore?
Because they don't want to wake the rest of the bunch.

☻

700. How can you easily pass a geometry test?
Know all the angles.

☻

701. What is an American vampire's favourite holiday?
Fangsgiving.

☻

702. What goes 'Buzz, zzub, buzz, zzub?'

A bee stuck to a yo-yo.

❂

703. What steals bubbles from a bath?
A robber duck.

❂

704. What do you get if you cross a clown with a pair of knickers?
Jester drawers.

❂

705. How was business for the man who sold lions to zoos?
He was doing a roaring trade.

❂

706. Where do private detectives do their shopping?
At a *snooper*market.

❂

707. What do you call a man who steals a cut of meat from a butcher's shop?
A chop lifter.

❂

708. What is small, furry, and used to chase outlaws in America?
A posse cat.

❂

709. Why did the bees go on strike?
Because they wanted shorter flowers and more honey.

❂

710. What happened when the computer fell on the floor?
It slipped a disk.

❂

711. What famous detective liked bubble baths?
Sherlock Foams.

❂

712. Why did the vampire's girlfriend tell him to use mouthwash?
Because he had bat breath.

❂

713. Why was the baby cat playing with the bandages?
Because it wanted to be a first aid kit.

❂

714. What has to be taken before you can get it?
A photograph.

❀

715. What is at the back of a bee?
It's bee-hind.

❀

716. What jackets can't you wear?
Jacket potatoes.

❀

717. What does an Eskimo use to keep his house together?
Ig-glue.

❀

718. What type of colourful bow is impossible to untie?
A rainbow.

❀

719. Who can hold up trains without being arrested?
Bridesmaids and pageboys.

❀

720. What was the name of the very first insect?
Adamant.

❀

721. What is green, slimy and hangs from trees?
Giraffe snot.

❀

722. Why did the razorbill raise 'er bill?
To let the sea-urchin see 'er chin.

❀

723. What do you get if you put your head in a bowl of an alcoholic fruit drink?
Punch up the nose.

❀

724. What goes: 'Dot, dash, dot, dot, croak'?
A morse toad.

❀

725. What is small, green, solves crimes and rubs its back legs together?
A grass copper.

❀

726. What sort of novels do birds like to read?
Trillers.

❀

727. What is worse than raining cats and dogs?
Hailing taxis.

✿

728. After a visit to the cinema, what did the vampire ask his girlfriend?
Do you want to go somewhere for a bite?

✿

729. What happened to the naughty witch at school?
She was ex-spelled.

✿

730. What is red, sticky and bites people in the neck?
A *jam*pire.

✿

731. What do you call twins who steal things?
A pair of nickers.

✿

732. Why did the cat give birth in a rubbish bin?
Because it read the notice on the side of the bin: 'Place your litter here.'

✿

733. What do you get if you cross a bee with a handbell?
A humdinger.

✿

734. Why do gorillas have such large nostrils?
Because they have large fingers.

✿

735. What do you call a hippo that jumps around on one leg?
A hoppo.

✿

736. What is very tall and smelly?
A skunk on stilts.

✿

737. What do you call an exploding sheep?
Baa-boom!

✿

738. What do female sheep wear in school?
Ewe-niforms.

✿

739. What can you hold without touching it?
A conversation.

❀

740. What's it like to be kissed by a vampire?
It's a pain in the neck.

❀

741. What is black and white and bounces up and down?
A penguin on a pogo stick.

❀

742. What is furry, white and smells of peppermint?
A polo bear.

❀

743. What do you call a very small person who likes travelling on the Paris underground while making a constant beat?
A Metro-gnome.

❀

744. What is quite large, male, has antlers and sucks blood?
A *moose*quito.

❀

745. What type of large cat will you always find in a library?
A catalogue.

❀

746. What do you call a large royal ape in prison?
King Kongvict.

❀

747. What do you call an ant that can't speak?
A mutant.

❀

748. Why was the spider ill?
Because it caught a nasty bug.

❀

749. Why did everyone in the courtroom keep jumping up and down?
Because it was a kangaroo court.

❀

750. What walks on a tightrope in the circus, does somersaults and says 'meow'?
An acro*cat*.

❀

751. What do you call a Japanese piano that keeps telling jokes?

A Yamaha-ha.

❀

752. What goes 'quack, quack, boom'?

A duck in a mine field.

❀

753. What carries a basket, goes through the woods, visits grandma and steals money?

Little Red Robin Hood.

❀

754. What flies but doesn't go anywhere when it's up?

A flag.

❀

755. What is the most use when it is used up?

An umbrella.

❀

756. What is it when a bike suddenly starts to bite people?

The start of a vicious cycle.

❀

757. You break it when you say it. What is it?

Silence.

❀

758. What is black and white, has a beak, likes fish and is very noisy?

A penguin with a drum kit.

❀

759. What did one eye say to the other eye?

'Between you and me, something smells.'

❀

R

RAFFLE

760. Bill asked his friend Philip to buy a raffle ticket.

'What's the raffle for?' asked Philip.

'You know Fred in accounts?' asked Bill. Philip nodded. Bill continued: 'Fred and his wife died in a car crash last week so the raffle is for his children.'

'Why,' asked Philip, 'would I want to buy such a raffle ticket? I'm already supporting three children of my own – I certainly don't want to win any more.'

❁

RELIGION

761. How can a priest keep fit?

Exorcise regularly.

❁

762. There I was in the desert, walking about all alone. Then I heard a voice saying: 'Yea, though I walk through the valley of the shadow of death, I will fear no evil.'

I looked around. No one. Not even a camel.

The voice continued: 'For thou art with me, thy rod and thy staff they comfort me.'

Then I realised the voice was coming from a tree near a small oasis. It was a psalm tree.

❁

763. What did John The Baptist and Winnie The Pooh have in common?

Their middle names.

❁

764. I can't understand those people who say they have just found God – I didn't know He was lost.

❁

765. Just before my youngest daughter was due to attend her first church service I told her what to expect: 'You have to put your hands together and then, at the end of a prayer, you say "Amen".'

'And after that', said my daughter, 'I put my arms out and say 'Arm out' and then 'Arm in'.

❀

RESTAURANTS AND CAFÉS

766. I went to a restaurant the other day and when the waiter brought me the menu I asked him: 'What do you recommend?'

He said: 'The restaurant just around the corner.'

❀

767. Keith had let his girlfriend choose the restaurant for a meal to celebrate their first six months together. When the waiter handed him a menu he was shocked at the prices of the food and wine. He looked at his girlfriend, stroked her under her chin and said: 'Well, my little plump one, let's keep a clear head for a night of passion.'

❀

768. I was in a restaurant recently and I overheard a man ask the waiter: 'How do you prepare the chicken?'

The waiter replied: 'Well, we sit the chicken down calmly, give it a sip of whisky and then say to it: "I'm sorry, but you're going to have to die".'

❀

769. A woman went into a café and ordered a meal. Then she changed her mind about her soup order and called for the waiter.

'I've decided to have the pea soup, instead of the turtle soup,' she said.

It was at that point a customer walked into the café and was astonished to hear the waiter shout to the chef: 'Hold the turtle. Make it pea.'

❀

770. When the waiter came towards me carrying my meal I noticed he was pressing two of his fingers down on to my fish.

'Excuse me,' I said to the waiter: 'It's not very hygienic putting your fingers on my food.'

'Well,' said the waiter, 'it's better than the fish falling off the plate on to the floor again.'

❀

771. When he went to a restaurant and saw that it displayed a notice: 'Ties Must Be Worn', he thought he would be refused admission as his tie was brand new and not worn.

❀

772. A gay couple were celebrating their tenth anniversary together by having a romantic meal in an expensive restaurant. However, the atmosphere was rather spoilt by a man and a woman at the next table having a fierce argument.

'See,' said one of the gay men, 'I told you mixed marriages can have problems.'

❀

RETIREMENT

773. I know a lot of men who took early retirement. Some of them laze around all day and put on weight. Their wives say that for them retirement means twice the husband but half the income.

❀

RUGBY

774. Nigel likes to play rugby – even though it's a very rough game. After the match on Saturday he came home with three broken teeth, a torn ear and a broken nose. I wish he would give them back to the players he took them from.

❀

775. Hugh liked to play Rugby – despite frequently suffering injuries from the game. Whenever his team won a match he enjoyed celebrating with some of his fellow players. They usually visited a house of ill-repute for drinks and women.

One day Hugh was appalled to discover that his scrotum had turned green and smelly. He went to a doctor who examined him and said: 'You already have a cauliflower ear – now you also have what can best be termed as *brothel* sprouts.'

☻

776. Sally was taken to a rugby match by her boyfriend. It was the first time she had watched the game and when the crowd cheered one of the moves of the players she heard a female spectator shout. 'Great tackle!' so Sally shouted: 'Cute bottom!'

☻

S

SAFETY
777. People say there's safety in numbers. Quite right. A million lemmings can't possibly be wrong.

⊛

SALESMEN
778. When he won his firm's Salesman of the Year Award for the sixth year in succession he said he owed his success to continuing to let his clients beat him at golf.

⊛

779. One door-to-door vacuum cleaner salesman consistently beat all sales records. His boss therefore decided to accompany the salesman to see what sales techniques he was using in the hope of being able to persuade others to use them.

The first door the salesman knocked on was opened by a middle-aged woman. 'Good morning,' said the salesman, 'Yesterday I visited one of your neighbours and I was demonstrating this vacuum cleaner when she told me a lot of interesting gossip. Would you like me to come in and tell you what she said?'

⊛

780. Yesterday a man knocked on my door and tried to sell me a lawn mower. I told him to visit my neighbour instead – I'm always borrowing his mower and it's time he got a better one I could borrow.

⊛

781. The salesman believed that to find out if honesty was the best policy he had to try all the other options first.

⊛

782. He's such a great salesman that when he takes a girl up to see his etchings he not only manages to have sex but sells her some of the etchings.

⊛

SATANIST

783. The Satanist who had difficulty with his spelling ended up selling his soul to Santa.

☻

SCHOOL

784. His daughter came home from school in tears. 'It's that horrible Mrs Robinson,' she sobbed. 'I spent hours and hours doing my homework and then, when I handed it in, she snapped at me and said: 'When I told you to make a relief map, I did *not* want a map showing the locations of public toilets!'

☻

785. He was so unloved at school that when he asked to join the marching band they gave him a grand piano.

☻

786. The teacher asked her young pupils to tell her something about their families. Little Rodney astonished the teacher by telling her that his mother hung around street corners stopping men and asking them questions.

The teacher was relieved to hear from Rodney's mother that she worked part-time as a market researcher.

☻

787. As a small boy I used to like maths until we had to do algebra. To me, it was a weapon of *math* destruction.

☻

788. The school bell rang and the teenage students started to get up from their seats.

'Wait!' shouted their female teacher. 'I just want to remind you of the test tomorrow. I expect all of you to attend. No excuses will be accepted – unless a member of your immediate family dies between now and the test – or you suffer a major injury.'

'But miss,' said a tall male student, 'what if someone suffers extreme sexual exhaustion?'

Some of the students giggled. But the teacher looked at the male student and said: 'If it was you, I would still expect you to do the test – but write with your other hand.'

☻

789. The school teacher asked: 'How many days of the week start with the letter "T"?'

Clarissa eagerly put up her hand and said: 'Two, miss.'

'That's right,' said the teacher. 'Very good. Now can you tell me the names of those two days that start with a T?'

'Of course,' replied Clarissa. 'Today and Tomorrow.'

☙

790. The teacher asked him: 'What is a bar chart?' He replied: 'A graph showing the decibel level of the voices of sheep.'

☙

791. 'Now,' said the school teacher, 'who can tell me what it means if you find a horseshoe?'

Christy put up her hand and said: 'I can miss. If you find a horseshoe it means a poor horse is having to limp. On one of its feet it has only got a sock.'

☙

792. The school teacher asked James: 'How many letters are there in the alphabet?'

James replied: 'Eleven.'

Puzzled, the teacher asked: '*Why* do you think the alphabet only has eleven letters?'

'Easy,' replied James. 'T.H.E. A.L.P.H.A.B.E.T. – that's eleven letters.'

☙

793. The head teacher at a junior school had prepared her pupils to give a show to the parents. The school choir and the school band would perform, several of the pupils would give individual performances of ballet and tap dancing, while others would recite poems or take part in a short play.

However, on the day of the performance, the head teacher realised she had overlooked one pupil – Henry. He had only been transferred to the school that morning and so had not had time to rehearse anything. Brought up on a farm, Henry and his parents had just moved to the city. She did not want to leave Henry out of the show – but what could he do?

'Henry?' asked the head teacher. 'Do you have a short poem or something you can recite in the show?'

'No, miss,' replied Henry. 'But I could do farmyard noises.'

'That would be great,' said the teacher.

The show seemed to be a great success. The parents wildly applauded the first few songs and dances and poetry recitals – but then came Henry. The small boy walked up to the microphone and solemnly announced: 'Farmyard noises.' Then, in a variety of voices, he yelled: 'Shut that bloody gate!' 'Go and bring the effing cows in for milking.' 'Get off that effing tractor!' 'Stop trampling on the bloody corn!' 'Stop chasing the effing chickens!' 'Who brought that bloody piglet into the house and let it shit everywhere?'

✿

794. When the teacher asked Claudia: 'What is protein?' Claudia replied: 'Isn't that the political party that's in favour of increased rights for teenagers?'

✿

795. The teacher began the lesson by saying: 'Rotting food, take-away cartons, empty boxes, used tissues, broken bottles, crumpled cardboard . . .'

'Oh dear,' whispered one pupil to her friend, 'He's talking garbage again.'

✿

796. 'Please miss,' said George to his teacher. 'There's a dead cat in the playground.'

'Oh dear,' replied the teacher. 'That's sad. Are you sure it is dead?'

'Yes, miss,' said George. 'It was just lying there on its side, not moving. So I pissed in its ear and . . .'

The horrified teacher interrupted him: 'You did *what*?'

George replied: 'I pissed in its ear. I bent over it and said "psssst".'

✿

797. I'm fed up with school,' said Emily. 'How do the teachers expect us to learn when they can never make up their minds.'

'What do you mean?' asked Emily's mother.

'On Monday,' said Emily, 'the teacher told us that two plus seven makes nine. Then on Tuesday she said that three plus six makes nine. And today she *still* wasn't sure of the right answer as she said five plus four makes nine.'

❀

798. When the teacher asked John to recite his tables he said: 'Dining table, coffee table, bedside table and kitchen table.'

❀

799. When he was at school he was voted the kid who would go far – everywhere he went he would be so hated they'd chase him away.

❀

800. A schoolteacher asked my young cousin: 'If you had £8.70 in one pocket and £9.30 in another pocket, what would you have?'

My cousin replied: 'Someone else's clothes.'

❀

801. The teacher asked the female pupil: 'Can you give me an example of the meaning of the word "congenital"?'

'Yes, miss,' replied the girl. 'When a young man rolls up several handkerchiefs and stuffs them down the front of his swimming trunks that's a *con*-genital.'

❀

802. When the young children went back to school after the summer holidays, they found they had all been moved up a class. 'Now, do you know what that means?' asked Vincent's teacher. 'It means that you are growing up and should no longer use babytalk. Did you all have a nice holiday?'

'Yes, miss,' chorused the children.

'Would someone like to tell me what they did?' asked the teacher. 'How about you, Amy?'

'Well, miss,' said Amy. 'My mum and dad and me went to visit a farm and we saw moo-moos and lots of baa-baas.'

'You mean cows and sheep,' said the teacher. 'Remember what I said earlier – you must use more adult language. Now, Vincent, what did you do on holiday?'

'I . . . I . . . I read a book,' stuttered a very nervous Vincent.

'That's good,' said the teacher. 'And what was the name of the book?'

'It was . . . it was . . . ' began Vincent, trying to remember that he had to talk more like an adult. 'It was, *Winnie The Shit*.

❁

803. He was so unpopular at school that when he played hide-and-seek no one came to find him.

❁

SCOTSMEN
804. How many budgerigars can fit under a Scotsman's kilt?

It depends on the length of the perch.

❁

SECRETS
805. If you must tell a secret to someone, tell it to an egotist. They won't pass on the secret because they are always so busy only talking about themselves.

❁

806. Of course I can keep secrets – it's the people I tell them to who can't.

❁

SELF-MADE
807. When he told me he was a self-made man I said it was very honest of him to take all the blame.

❁

808. If he's a self-made man, why did he make himself look so ugly?

❁

809. He was a self-made man. Unfortunately, he quit before he'd finished.

❁

SEX

810. He believes that sex is like everything else – if you want it done right, don't get others to do it: do it yourself.

❀

811. Their love-making was fast and furious – he was too fast and she was furious.

❀

812. Brian was desperate for sex, so went to town looking for some. Due to his poor ability at reading he ended up spending a night in a warehouse.

❀

813. She *loves* money – she only has sex in the *mercenary* position.

❀

814. Last night he picked up a girl at the local nightclub and took her back to his apartment. After a quick session of sex she put her clothes on and said: 'I don't think we should see each other again.'

'Why not?' he asked.

'Well,' she said, 'I don't know how to put this politely, but your organ isn't large enough.'

'Oh!' he replied. 'It wasn't designed to be played in a cathedral.'

❀

815. He said that sex with his wife was like visiting a late night grocery store in a small town: the goods were not very attractive, there was little variety and they cost a lot – but there was nothing else available after 10.30pm.

❀

816. His wife says he's an animal in bed – a sloth.

❀

817. Last night in a bar I overheard a man talking to a young woman. He said: 'Having sex with my wife is like Valentine's Day.'

The woman said: 'That sounds as if it's wonderfully romantic.'

'No,' replied the man, 'It only happens once a year.'

❀

818. He's one of the world's greatest lovers. He loves the world – but in bed he's hopeless.

✿

819. Jeremy and his wife are sexually compatible – every night they both have headaches.

✿

820. Clive was in a bar, having a quiet drink with some of his friends. Suddenly, a man lurched into the bar, looked at Clive and shouted: 'I've just had sex with your mother!' Then he ran out of the bar.

Clive blushed and his friends tried hard not to smirk. They continued their drinking for another hour or so until the same man came back into the bar and shouted at Clive: 'We've done it again! She may be old, with droopy boobs, but she's still got stamina. Sex with your mother was fantastic!'

One of Clive's friends whispered to Clive: 'If you want, I'll help you take him outside and give him a beating. What he's shouting is disgusting!'

Clive, embarrassed, said to the man who had shouted at him: 'Please leave me alone. I know it's very rare for you to have sex – but there's no need to shout about it. I'll meet you outside and we can talk quietly about it when I've finished my drink, Dad.'

✿

821. His wife told him he should be much more loving – so he went and got two mistresses.

✿

822. They have sex doggie fashion – he has to beg for it and then she rolls over and plays dead.

✿

823. Brian says that he has sex almost every day. That means he *almost* has it on Mondays, *almost* on Tuesdays, *almost* on Wednesdays . . .

✿

824. Women say that a good sense of humour is vital in a relationship – that's why he doesn't mind when his wife laughs at him while they make love.

✿

825. The hen-pecked husband turned to his wife after making love and said: 'I hope that was great for you – how was it for me?'

❁

826. His wife complained about his love-making. He protested: 'Why don't you ever tell me when you're about to reach orgasm.'

'Because,' she replied, 'you're never there.'

❁

827. What do girls who have sex on the first date usually do after sex? Open the window of the car door to get some air.

❁

828. When choosing a sexual partner women should remember that it is not the length of the wand that matters most – but how much magic it can do.

❁

829. What words do you most fear hearing when you're making love to a woman?

'Honey, I'm home.'

❁

830. In order to try to improve their pay and conditions the town's prostitutes came to a grinding halt.

❁

831. The young Chinese couple were in bed when the man said: 'How about trying 69?'

His girlfriend was surprised, but snuggled up to him and said: 'I'd love 69 – but can't we make love some more before we order the stir fried king prawns with mixed vegetables in oyster sauce?'

❁

832. Someone once asked her if drugs were better than sex. She said it depended on the pusher.

❁

833. Charles had gone abroad on a business trip. He missed his wife, so he phoned her and said: 'Darling, let's have phone sex.'

'Not tonight, dear,' she replied. 'I've got earache.'

❁

SHOPPING

834. When she went to a shop to get a deodorant for her husband, the sales assistant asked: 'Ball type?'

'No,' she replied, 'It's for his armpits.'

❀

835. The elderly gentleman stepped out of the Rolls Royce, a doorman smartly opened the doors of the department store and the man made his way to one of the perfume counters. He rested his hands on the counter and the young sales assistant noticed his expensive watch and rings.

'I hope you can help me,' said the elderly gentleman. 'What can you suggest for a man of ninety-six?'

The young sales assistant smiled sweetly and said: 'How about a young woman of twenty-two?'

❀

836. Whenever he goes out with his wife he holds her hand. That way he hopes to be able to steer her away from expensive shops.

❀

837. She went to a general store – she thought they might sell her a military man.

❀

838. I was in a card shop just before Valentine's Day and I saw a man buy over a hundred Valentine's cards.

'You must have a lot of girlfriends,' I said.

'No,' he replied. 'I send them to people who I know are married. I use the cards to help expand my business. I'm a divorce lawyer.'

❀

839. If someone is ill and you go to a card shop and look at their display of Get Well cards you will find that most of them say 'Get Well Soon'. Why do they need the word 'soon'? Surely by wishing someone to 'Get Well' you want them to get better as quickly as possible? Or maybe there's a range of cards in a bottom drawer for people you hate which state: 'Get Well Slowly'?

❀

840. The middle-aged man was walking anxiously up and down the aisles in a large supermarket.

Then he saw a very attractive woman, so he went to her and said: 'Can I talk to you for twenty seconds?'

The woman looked at him and asked: 'Why?'

The man explained: 'I came here shopping with my wife, but I can't find her. I'm fed up with walking up and down all the aisles looking for her. But I know that as soon as I talk to an attractive woman, my wife will magically appear, silently standing behind me.'

❁

841. The famous rock star was tired of getting mobbed by fans and hounded by the press, so he decided to change his appearance when he ventured out to do some Christmas shopping. He got his make up artist to give his face pimples and scars, and he wore old, unattractive clothes and walked with a limp.

He had an enjoyable morning, paying cash for all his purchases as he had deliberately not taken his cheque book or credit cards with him as it would be too easy to reveal his identity.

After a pleasant lunch, the rock star continued his shopping. In a jewellery store he discovered a uniquely designed pendant that would be ideal for one of his girlfriends. But when he went to pay for it, he discovered he had run out of cash.

'Could you keep the pendant for an hour or so until I can return with some cash?' asked the rock star.

'How do I know you will return?' asked the sales assistant. 'I don't want to appear unkind, but we get many people asking to put items aside and then they never return.'

'I promise I will return,' said the rock star.

'Well, I don't know,' said the sales assistant.

'Look,' said the rock star, 'I'm really quite a famous singer but I've dressed down as I wanted to do my shopping without being pestered by fans and the press.'

The sales assistant looked doubtful, so the rock singer revealed his name. The sales assistant said: 'Do you have any proof? You don't look like him. If you are who you say you are, could you sing a bit of your latest hit?'

'What?' said the rock star. 'Sing without a microphone – or my backing singers and musicians? I couldn't possibly do that.'

'OK,' said the shop assistant. 'I'll save the pendant for you. You've just proved who you are.'

❀

SHORT
842. If you don't stop telling jokes about my shortness of height I'll bite you in the knees.

❀

843. It's really unfair. Short men are just called short – but short women are called petite.

❀

SIGNS
844. When he saw a sign that said 'Say No To Crack' he pulled his trousers up higher.

❀

SLEEP
845. One of the great mysteries of life is why is it that when you share a bedroom, the person who goes to sleep first is always the one who snores?

❀

846. Her husband awoke from a deep sleep and said to her: 'Please turn off the TV and let's have a drink and go to bed.'

She replied: 'I'm sorry, dear, that's not possible. We're still at the opera house.'

❀

SMOKING
847. When I first gave up smoking it reminded me of my first visit to a nudist camp – I was at a bit of a loss to know what to do with my hands.

❀

SNEEZING

848. A friend of mine told me that every time she sneezed she had an orgasm. I asked her if she was taking anything for it.

'Yes,' she said. 'Lots of pepper.'

❁

SPEECHES

849. His speeches are so boring he puts more people to sleep than an anaesthetist.

❁

850. I have a slight impediment in my speech – my lawyer won't allow me to say anything.

❁

851. She started her speech at 10 am sharp – and ended it at 11.30 am dull.

❁

852. He's a man of few words – it's a great pity he repeats them for hours.

❁

853. He can talk in public for hours without a note – and usually without a point.

❁

854. A toastmaster is the person who starts the bull rolling.

❁

855. He is well-known for his boring speeches. But as he is chairman of a large company he is sometimes asked to speak at business dinners and conferences. The organisers of such events are attracted by his status rather than his speaking ability.

However, last night at a business function he started off by asking: 'Can you hear me at the back of the room?' And a voice from the back shouted: 'Yes. But I'd be pleased to change places with someone who can't.'

❁

856. At the end of his speech he left his audience open-mouthed – they all yawned at the same time.

❁

SPONTANEOUS

857. Last night I saw him making a list of things to do today. The thirtieth item on his list was: 'Be more spontaneous.'

❀

SPORTS

858. My hobby is booing millionaires – I go to a top football club's match and boo the players.

❀

859. Football is the favourite game of men working on the assembly line in the factory, or in a clerical position in the office.

Squash or tennis are the favourite sports of middle-managers.

Chairmen, directors and executives love playing golf.

This proves that the higher a man is on the corporate ladder, the smaller his balls.

❀

860. His baseball team are known as The Scrambled Eggs – they are always getting beaten.

❀

861. One day, after winning a particularly hard game of tennis, Malcolm picked up several of the balls and absent-mindedly put them in the pockets of his shorts. Then he went to the bar for a drink.

Sitting at the bar was a young woman. She looked at the bulge in his shorts and her eyes widened.

Malcolm followed her gaze, blushed with embarrassment and said: 'It's only tennis balls.'

'Oh,' said the woman. 'That must be rather painful. When I had tennis elbow it ached for a month.'

❀

862. She used to be an all-round sportswoman but as she got older she just became all-round.

❀

STRESS

863. I recently went on a stress management course. Now I fully understand the real cause of stress – it's management.

❀

STUDENTS

864. The student was trying to save money in order to go on a foreign holiday so she got a Saturday job in a local chemist's shop. On her first day at work a man came in wanting to buy a thermometer. 'What one would you recommend?' asked the customer.

The girl picked up several boxes of thermometers, looked at them and said: 'Well, I know people think German products are reliable so I suggest you get the Fahrenheit one.'

❁

865. How do male students sort their clothes?

Into three piles: might be clean, dirty but wearable, and dirty and smelly.

❁

866. The male students at the university consider a balanced diet to be a beer in one hand and a pie in the other hand.

❁

867. University students believe there are three main food groups – frozen, canned and take-away.

❁

868. One applicant for a media studies course was asked by a university tutor: 'If you could interview anyone, living or dead, who would you interview?'

The applicant replied: 'The living one.'

❁

SUNDIAL

869. He recently painted the sundial in his garden. He used luminous paint because he said he wanted to be able to tell the time at night.

❁

T

TALK

870. When she is alone in bed, Alison talks to her vagina and it talks back to her. She says it's her answering cervix.

❀

TAX

871. The greatest difference between death and taxes is that death doesn't get worse every time the government presents its Budget.

❀

872. The problem with income tax forms is that it takes more time and effort to fill in the forms than it does to earn the income.

❀

TELEKINESIS

873. All those who believe in telekinesis raise *my* right hand.

❀

TELEVISION

874. When she told me she wanted to appear on TV as a weather woman I said it was a good idea. The audience would have to guess whether she's a woman.

❀

875. The reason they call the TV control a 'remote' is that with a sports mad husband in the house and five teenage children a wife has a remote chance of controlling the channel.

❀

876. One of the most annoying things about getting older is the TV programmes. I am sick of seeing shows where experts say how certain toys, furniture, ornaments and stuff are now so valuable, but originally were very cheap.

The shows really depress me as the items they talk about are those which people my age used to own – but long ago threw away.

⊛

877. The ratings of a TV late-night current affairs interview series had plummeted. There were calls from the press and certain people within the TV organisation to cancel the show.

The researchers, producers, directors and presenters were naturally worried they might soon be made redundant and held a meeting to discuss the reasons for the fall in ratings and what could be done to improve the show.

'Viewers have gone off the main presenters,' said a brave researcher. 'Whereas one of the presenters used to be just mildly pompous – now many viewers think that he is also arrogant and condescending and just switch off.'

'Nonsense!' snapped a presenter. 'The problem is the quality of research. I'm frequently given notes that are wrong. What I want are clear signs of whether or not someone I'm interviewing is lying – then, if I've got firm proof, I can really attack him and call him a liar to his face.'

'I think I can help,' said a technician. 'My father is an award-winning scientist and he has been studying human behaviour for years. I'm sure that, for an appropriate fee, he could invent something that could spot the signs that someone is lying and indicate that to the interviewer.'

The senior producer thought the technician's idea was a good one and so the scientist was contracted to create a suitable lie detector.

After several weeks of feverish activity, the scientist produced a chair that looked exactly like all the other chairs used by people being interviewed on the show. But, hidden inside the chair, were complicated monitoring systems that checked changes in the body temperature, sweat rate, pulse, tenseness, changes in tone of voice and a whole host of other factors that would indicate whether or not someone sitting in the chair was giving a lying answer to a question.

To indicate to the presenter the severity of the lie, the chair would give the person being interviewed a very mild electric shock. The person would then give a slight, almost unnoticeable twitch for which the presenter should be alert. The worse the lie, the greater the shock – which would have the added advantage of causing the interviewee to feel somewhat uncomfortable so he or she might then start to make obvious mistakes. The shocks might even provoke lying interviewees into fits of anger – which would be especially good for the ratings. No one would suspect that the chair was responsible for the shocks.

Everyone was delighted with the chair. One of the presenters was chosen to test it. When he was sitting comfortably he was asked: 'What is the capital of England?' When he replied: 'Edinburgh', he gave a small twitch.

Watching a replay of the tape of his questioning, the presenter said the shock was so mild he had not been conscious of the twitch it provoked.

The production team were ecstatic. They decided to put the chair into use on that evening's show when a prominent politician was due to be interviewed about the Government's policies.

Thus it was that the repeat screenings of that interview attracted record ratings all around the world. The interviewer asked the politician an opening easy question and the politician began: 'I think . . .' – and the chair and the politician exploded in a burst of sparks and flames.

☺

THEATRE
878. His latest theatre production had a happy ending. When the final curtain came, the audience were happy that the boring play had ended.

☺

879. He's fresh from his success with a one man show – only one man showed up to see it.

✿

TIME
880. The length of a minute depends on whether you are the one doing the waiting, or are the one for whom other people are waiting.

✿

TIREDNESS
881. Agnes was tending to her houseplants when she realised that she felt rather tired and droopy. 'Perhaps,' she mused to herself, 'I need re-potting.'

✿

TORCHES
882. Whenever we have an electricity blackout it's then I discover that every torch in the house is just a useful container for storing dead batteries.

✿

TOWN
883. In this town you know what pretty girls and handsome men are – tourists!

✿

TREES
884. I've often wondered what happens if a tree falls in a forest and no one hears it fall. Who notifies the next of kindling?

✿

U

URINALS
885. One of the fascinations for him of men's urinals used to be the writing on the wall. But he stopped reading the jokes and slogans after seeing a notice stating: 'Why are you looking at this wall? The joke is in your hand.'

✿

V

VEGETARIANS
886. Of course I've got nothing against vegetarians. I eat lots of vegetables and green stuff – it's just that I prefer to eat the animals after they've processed it.

✿

887. If vegetarians eat vegetables, why don't humanitarians eat people?

✿

VENTRILOQUIST
888. The ventriloquist sat on the stage with his dummy – a small, wooden boy with a large head. His act was not going well. In desperation, he started to tell jokes about people from a country that shall remain nameless.

This enraged one woman in the audience, who shouted. '*Stop it*! How *dare* you tell such jokes. I'm from that country and the people are nowhere near as stupid as you make out.'

The ventriloquist was very apologetic. 'I'm sorry,' he said. 'I was just . . .'

The woman snapped: '*Shut up*! I wasn't talking to *you*! I was talking to that large headed boy on your lap.'

✿

W

WARS
889. Wars do not decide who is right . . . they determine who is left.

❀

WATCHES AND CLOCKS
890. She was so keen to show off the expensive watch which her rich boyfriend had given her that she wore it to work.

It was noon and no one had asked her about her watch. She raised her hand above her head and waggled her wrist in the hope that at least one of her office colleagues would see the glittering watch and ask her about it. Still nothing.

Then she stood up, looked at her watch and said in a loud voice: 'If anyone is interested in the time it's almost one ruby past the large diamond.'

❀

891. If a cuckoo pops out of a cuckoo clock, why doesn't a grandfather pop out of a grandfather clock?

❀

892. He's just bought a Prime Minister watch. It's got two faces.

WEDDINGS
893. I'd like to thank my Uncle Paul for the wonderful wedding present of a 50-piece dinner set. The box of wooden toothpicks will be really useful.

❀

894. When the actress was asked why she had candles on her wedding cake, she replied: 'Well, it *is* an annual event.'

❀

895. It was a strange wedding. The bride was so ugly that all the men kissed the groom instead.

❀

896. This is a very emotional wedding – even the cake is in tiers.

❀

897. When my young son found the photo album of my wedding he brought it to me and asked: 'Is this when mummy agreed to come and work for us?'

❀

898. On the day before her wedding the bride-to-be was given some advice by her mother: 'If you give a man an inch or a centimetre he'll think he's a ruler.'

❀

899. His wife has still got her wedding outfit – the beautiful white dress, the veil – and the shotgun.

❀

900. It was a typical wedding – the bride looked stunning and the groom appeared stunned.

❀

901. Unfortunately, Aunt Doris is unable to attend the wedding. But she has sent a nice card of congratulation and a present. She would like me to send her – and I quote: 'A photo of the bride and groom mounted.'

❀

902. I would like to thank my mother-in-law for the wonderful present – a set of towels marked 'Hers' and 'Thing'.

❀

903. If you are single, the chances are that if you attend a relative's wedding various aunts and uncles will come up to you, poke you in the ribs and cackle: '*You'll* be the next!'

One way to stop them from continuing this habit is to go to a relative's funeral and poke the aunts and uncles in the ribs and say to them: 'Oh dear, *you* might be the next.'

❀

WEDDING ANNIVERSARY

904. When Lionel woke up on the morning of his tenth wedding anniversary he immediately burst into tears.

'What's wrong, dear?' asked his wife, Eileen. 'You should be happy – we've been together ten wonderful years. Let's make love to celebrate.'

Lionel looked at her pock-marked face, her large nose, triple chin, cauliflower ears and her grotesquely huge body and cried even louder.

'Remember,' he sobbed, 'when I was senior accountant to your brother's firm?'

'Yes, dear,' said Eileen, patting him with one of her pudgy hands.

'Well,' continued Lionel, between sobs, 'he discovered that I had embezzled a lot of money from the firm. I had gambled it away on betting on horses and investing in shares in companies that went bust. He described you to me and explained that you were having great difficulty in finding a man to love. He said that if I married you he wouldn't report me to the police. If they had been called in I would have gone to prison. If he had done that, the prison sentence I would have been given would probably have expired today – and I would now be a free man.'

☙

905. On their fiftieth wedding anniversary, her husband kissed her and said: 'I wonder what happened to our sexual relations.'

She replied: 'I don't know. They never reply, even though I send them a card every Christmas.'

☙

906. The couple had just celebrated their fiftieth wedding anniversary. Just as they were about to go to bed, a fairy suddenly appeared and said: 'I am a good fairy. You have both been such a good couple for so many years that I can grant you one wish each.'

The fairy turned to the wife and asked: 'What would you like?'

'A sack full of money,' said the woman. There was a puff of smoke and the sack of money appeared. The woman was delighted and started to count the money.

Her husband approached the fairy and whispered: 'For my wish, I would like to have a woman much younger than me.'

There was a puff of smoke, and the man found himself lying on the floor. He was twenty years older.

❀

907. Doris and Derek were an elderly married couple. As a sixtieth wedding anniversary present one of their sons had given them the latest in satellite television systems. It had a motorised dish which meant the TV could pick up TV programmes from all around the world.

One evening, while flicking around the channels, Doris discovered a preacher who claimed to have healing powers.

'Come and look at this!' called Doris to her husband. 'This man on TV says that if we put a hand on the part of the body that ails us, then we can be healed. I'm going to put my hands on my knees – maybe the preacher will help my rheumatism.'

Derek stood watching the program and put his hand into his trousers. Doris saw what he was doing and said: 'I'm sorry, dear, but the preacher said he could heal, not raise the dead.'

❀

WEIGHT
908. When I was asked how my stomach grew so large, I said it must have just *snacked* up on me.

❀

909. She realised she was rather fat when she gave one of her dresses to a charity shop and a group of scouts bought it to use as a tent.

❀

910. I know I've put on a lot of weight. I used to weigh 3.5 kilograms.

❀

911. I didn't think I was fat until last summer. It was a hot sunny day and I wanted to sunbathe in the garden. When I asked my wife to put suntan lotion on my back she said she would go to the garage and get something that would make it easier to apply the lotion. She came back from the garage with a paint roller.

❀

912. My husband is so fat they refused to let him go bungee jumping off the local bridge – they thought he might make it collapse.

❀

913. Hermione booked herself into a health farm for two weeks in order to lose weight. While at the farm she had her fortieth birthday. Several of her friends sent her some flowers. Hermione responded with 'thank you' notes stating that the flowers were 'delicious'.

❀

914. The best way to lose weight is not to exceed the feed limit.

❀

915. If swimming is supposed to be a good way of losing weight – then why are whales so huge?

❀

916. Mrs Jones and her daughter lived next door to a very nosy old man. He was always looking out of his windows, or standing in his garden peering over the fence.

One day he said to Mrs Jones: 'Your daughter seems to be putting on a bit of weight.'

'Yes,' replied Mrs Jones. 'It's a hormonal thing with teenagers.'

Soon it appeared that the old man was obsessed with the girl's weight.

One day he said: 'Your daughter's stomach really seems to have grown. She's sixteen, isn't she?'

'Yes,' replied Mrs Jones. 'But she's been suffering from wind. Her tummy is just a bit bloated – but I expect it will eventually go down.'

Some time later the old man said: 'Your daughter still seems to have a problem with her tummy.'

'Yes,' replied Mrs Jones. 'It's just wind.'

A month later the old man noticed Mrs Jones's daughter in the garden, cuddling a small baby. 'Ah!' he said to Mrs Jones, 'Is that the little fart?'

❀

WILLS

917. My uncle in Canada told me that he would leave me a large sum in his will. Last month he passed away and the lawyer read the will. The large sum was: 1.5 million multiplied by 358.5 divided by 52.5 minus 10,242,852. (The sum was large – but when I went to collect the money I found the amount was small – only around $5).

❀

WIVES

918. He owes everything he has to his wife – his years of toiling in a boring job, his house with a huge mortgage, his delinquent children, his bank balance of zero, his ulcer – absolutely everything he owes to her!

❀

919. His wife has an even temper – she's always angry.

❀

920. Whatever happened, his wife always looked on the bright side. She was much more than an optimist – she was a hope addict.

❀

921. My wife is like a wild animal in bed – she snores like a hippo.

❀

922. His wife would look good in something long and flowing – like the Nile or the Amazon.

❀

923. He hasn't spoken to his wife for the past six months – she hates to be interrupted.

❀

924. He says he's fortunate that his wife's only extravagance is spending money.

❀

925. He's a very happy man with a wife who is fantastic in bed and a wife who cooks superb meals and does his laundry. He just hopes the two women never meet.

❀

926. He said he realised how much his wife loved him when he unexpectedly fell ill and could not go to work for three days. His wife was so pleased to have him at home that she told everyone about it. Every time the phone rang she started off by saying: 'My husband's at home.' When-ever anyone started walking up the path to his front door – such as the newspaper deliverer, milkman, mailman and gardener – she rushed out saying: 'My husband's at home!'

❂

927. I wouldn't say my wife is a witch – but she has a sticker in the rear window of her car stating: 'My other vehicle is a broom.'

❂

928. Every morning my wife likes something pink and hard – the *Financial Times* crossword.

❂

929. You can tell when his wife is starting to get tired – she can hardly keep her mouth open.

❂

930. He recently ordered a very expensive gag that was guaranteed impossible to remove by the person wearing it. He said it was money well spent as he'd have given anything for a quiet wife.

❂

931. When I told my wife I'd met a man who rowed across the Atlantic single-handed, she asked: 'Why didn't he use both hands?'

❂

932. My wife likes to pick up a good book and not put it down until she's finished. Unfortunately, it's my cheque book.

❂

933. The only time my wife pays any attention to what I am saying is when I talk in my sleep.

❂

934. He can talk to his wife about anything – politics, philosophy, music, sport, religion, books, art – absolutely anything. She won't understand it – but he can talk to her about it.

❂

935. My wife is very dear to me – with all the stuff she buys she costs me a fortune.

❂

936. Lots of women say they want a man's salary. My wife already gets one – she takes all of mine.

❁

937. When my wife was pregnant she was amazed at all the women in the street who would suddenly smile at her. I said it was because they were all delighted to see someone fatter than them.

❁

938. The only things his wife knows how to make for dinner are restaurant reservations.

❁

WOMEN
939. A woman who wants to be as successful as a man is a woman who lacks real ambition.

❁

940. The reason why women have at least two good friends is because they need at least one to talk *to* and one or more to talk *about*.

❁

941. She's the kind of woman that men look twice at – it needs the second look to confirm that it really is possible for someone to be that ugly.

❁

942. You shouldn't call her 'easy'. It's much more polite to say she's very accessible horizontally.

❁

943. Women are like a computer software package. Soon after you sign up to one a better model becomes available.

❁

944. She's so desperate for male attention that when she moved house she sent a change-of-address card to the Peeping Tom.

❁

945. For some men, the best women are like the best coffee – rich, hot and they keep you up.

❁

946. The only time she desires a man's company is when he owns one.

❁

947. When a woman is described as being 'easy' it just means that she has the same sexual morals as the average man.

❀

948. Someone once asked me what I first notice about a woman. I said it depends whether I'm walking behind her or she's walking towards me.

❀

949. The reason women generally have smaller feet than men is due to the evolutionary process. Smaller feet allow women to stand closer to the kitchen sink.

❀

950. What is the difference between a woman and a brick?
After you've laid one brick it doesn't mind if you lay another.

❀

951. A friend of mine recently told me that he loves women so much he thinks he must be a lesbian.

❀

952. Some women's breasts are rather like toys. They are designed for kids, but quite often it is the father who spends the most time playing with them.

❀

953. It's not women's minds that get some men excited – but what the women don't mind.

❀

954. What is the difference between a puppy and a woman?
The puppy will soon grow up and stop whining.

❀

955. He thinks the best shape for a woman is to have a narrow waist and a broad mind.

❀

956. The reason so few women break through the glass ceiling is because they know they'll get no help from men to pick up the pieces.

❀

WORDS

957. My sister thinks that a penal colony is a place for male nudists.

❀

958. A synonym is a word you use when you can't spell the word you really want.

❀

959. My young cousin thinks that a granary is a home for grandmothers.

❀

960. He thinks that an innuendo is an Italian suppository.

❀

961. He thinks that a teetotaller is someone who keeps the score during a game of golf.

❀

962. Why do people insist on using a big word when a diminutive one will suffice?

❀

Z

ZOO

963. He was lazing on the sofa, watching TV and drinking beer, when his wife told him to get up and take the children to the zoo. He took another sip of his beer, belched, and said to his wife: 'If the zoo wants the children I'm sure they'll bring a cage and come and collect them.'

❀

964. One of the healthiest animals in the zoo is the ant-eater. It's got lots of protection against diseases as it's full of anty-bodies.

❀

965. What is the difference between zoos in a country that shall be nameless and zoos in other parts of the world?

In normal zoos, each cage and enclosure is labelled with a brief description of the animals in it. In the country that shall be nameless, the description is accompanied by recipes.

❀